The LIFE ON OTHER WORLDS SERIES is a selection
of classic accounts of the afterlife and otherworldly
life, told by those who are already there or who have
been shown glimpses of what awaits us when our lives
on earth are over. Descriptions vary, yet a thread of
similarity runs through them all. May this collection
serve as a travel guide as we embark on the greatest
adventure of all—the journey into the mysterious
realms beyond this world.

*

OTHER VOLUMES IN THE SERIES INCLUDE
The Realms Beyond (1878) Paschal Beverly Randolph
A Wanderer in the Spirit Lands (1896) Franchezzo
Intra Muros (1898) Rebecca Ruter Springer
The Angels' Diary (1903) Effie M. Shirey
Two Years in Heaven (1911) Rose the Sunlight
The Life Beyond the Veil (4 Vols.) (1920-21) G. Vale Owen
Spiritual Life on Mars (1920) Eros Urides
The Blue Island & Other Spiritualist Writings (1922) William T. Stead
The World Unseen (3 Vols.) (1954-59) Anthony Borgia

EARTHS

in the

UNIVERSE

Their Spirits and Inhabitants

(1758)

Emanuel Swedenborg

SQUARE CIRCLES PUBLISHING

EARTHS IN THE UNIVERSE
Their Spirits and Inhabitants
Emanuel Swedenborg
(1758)

Cover: Syrp & Co.
Cover images: Wikimedia Commons / NASA imagery

SQUARE CIRCLES PUBLISHING
P. O. Box 9682 / Pahrump, NV 89060
www.SquareCircles.com
www.LifeOnOtherWorlds.com

ISBN: 978-0-9905813-1-4

Contents

Introduction

EMANUEL SWEDENBORG (1688-1772) was a Swedish scientist, philosopher, theologian, revelator, and mystic. In *Earths in the Universe* he claimed to converse with spirits from planets both within and without our solar system, concluding that the Infinite God would not create such an enormous undertaking for one world alone, with only one heaven for one race of people. Swedenborg says:

> That there are many worlds, may be evident to every one, from there being so many constellations visible in the universe; and it is known in the learned world that every fixed star is like a sun in its place . . . Consequently that like the sun of our world, it has round it planets, which are earths; and the reason that these do not appear to our eyes, is their being at such an immense distance, and having only the light of their star, which cannot be reflected again as far as here. For what other purpose is there so great a heaven with so many stars? For the end of the creation of the universe is man, that from man there may be an angelic heaven. [n.126]

Swedenborg devoted ten years to his eight-volume magnum opus, *Arcana Coelestia* (*Heavenly Mysteries*, or *Secrets of Heaven*), published between 1749 and 1756, which became the basis of his further theological works. The footnotes in *Earths in the Universe* refer to passages in that work.

SASKIA PRAAMSMA
Square Circles Publishing

ONE

Earths in the Universe

1 SINCE, FROM THE DIVINE MERCY OF THE LORD, THE INTERIORS, which are of my spirit, have been opened to me, and thereby it has been granted me to speak with spirits and angels, not only with those who are near our earth, but also with those who are near other earths; because I had a desire to know whether there are other earths, and what their nature is, and the quality of their inhabitants, therefore it has been granted me by the Lord to speak and converse with spirits and angels who are from other earths, with some for a day, with some for a week, and with some for months; and to be instructed by them concerning the earths, from which and near which they were; and concerning the lives, customs, and worship of the inhabitants thereof, and of various other things worthy to be related: and because in this manner it has been granted me to know these things, it is permitted to describe them from what has been heard and seen. It is to be known that all spirits and angels are from the human race;[1] and that they are near their own earths;[2] and that they know what is there; and that by them man may be instructed, if his

---

[1] (From the *Arcana Coelestia*, where this and the following notes are explained and shown.) There are no spirits and angels who are not from the human race (n. 1880).

[2] The spirits of every earth are near to their own earth, because they are from the inhabitants of that earth, and of a similar genius; and they are serviceable to those inhabitants (n. 9968).

interiors are so far opened that he can speak and converse with them; for man in his essence is a spirit,[3] and he is together with spirits as to his interiors;[4] wherefore he whose interiors are opened by the Lord, may speak with them as man with man;[5] which has been granted me now for twelve years daily.

2 That there are many earths, and men upon them, and spirits and angels thence, is well known in the other life, for it is there granted to every one who desires it from a love of truth, and thence of use, to speak with the spirits of other earths, and thereby to be confirmed concerning a plurality of worlds, and to be informed that the human race is not from one earth only, but from innumerable earths; and moreover to be informed what is their genius, manner of life, and their Divine worship.

3 I have occasionally spoken on this subject with the spirits of our earth, and it was said that any man of keen understanding may conclude from many things that he knows that there are many earths, and that there are men there; for it may be concluded from reason that such great masses as the planets are, some of which exceed this earth in magnitude, are not empty masses, and created only to be conveyed in their revolutions round the sun, and to shine with their scanty light for one earth, but that their use must needs be more excellent than that. He who believes, as every one ought to believe, that the Divine created the universe for no other end than that the human race may exist, and thence heaven, for the human race is the seminary of heaven, must needs believe also, that wherever there is an earth, there are men. That the planets which are visible to our eyes, as being within the boundaries of this solar system, are earths, may be manifestly known from this, that they are bodies of earthy matter, because they reflect the light of the sun, and when seen through optical glass-

---

[3] The soul, which lives after death, is the spirit of man, which is the real man in him, and also appears in the other life in a perfect human form (n. 322, 1880 1881, 3633, 4622, 4735, 6054, 6605, 6626, 7021, 10,594).
[4] Man, even when he is in the world, as to his interiors, thus as to his spirit or soul, is in the midst of spirits and angels, of a quality such as he is himself (n. 2379, 3645, 4067, 4073, 4077).
[5] Man can speak with spirits and angels, and the ancients on our earth frequently spoke with them (n. 67-69, 784, 1634, 1636, 7802). But at this day it is dangerous to speak with them, unless man is in true faith, and led by the Lord (n. 784, 9438, 10,751).

es, they appear, not as stars glittering by reason of their flame, but as earths variegated from darker portions. The same may further appear from this, that they, in like manner as our earth, are conveyed by a progressive motion round the sun, in the way of the zodiac, whence they have their years, and seasons of the year, as spring, summer, autumn, and winter; and in like manner, as our earth, revolve about their own axis, whence they have their days, and times of the day, as morning, noon, evening and night. Moreover some of them have moons, which are called satellites, and which revolve round their globes at stated times, as the moon does round our earth. Also the planet Saturn has besides a large luminous belt, because it is very far distant from the sun, which belt supplies that earth with much light, although reflected. Who that knows these things and from reason thinks about them can say that these are empty bodies?

4 Moreover, when I have spoken with spirits, I have said that men may believe that in the universe there are more earths than one, from this, that the starry heaven is so immense, and the stars therein are so innumerable, each of which in its place, or in its world, is a sun, and like our sun, in various magnitude. Whoever duly considers, concludes that so immense a whole must needs be a means to an end, which is the ultimate of creation, which end is the kingdom of heaven, wherein the Divine may dwell with angels and men; for the visible universe, or the heaven resplendent with stars so innumerable, which are so many suns, is only a means for the existence of earths, and of men upon them, of whom may be formed a heavenly kingdom. From these things a rational man must needs be led to conceive, that so immense a means, adapted to so great an end, was not constituted for a race of men and for a heaven thence derived from one earth only; for what would this be to the Divine, which is infinite, and to which thousands, yea, ten thousands of earths, all full of inhabitants, would be small and scarce anything.

5 Moreover, the angelic heaven is so immense, that it corresponds with all the particulars with man, myriads corresponding to every member, organ, and viscus, and to every affection of each; and it has been given to know, that this heaven, as to all its correspondences, can by no means exist, except from the inhabitants of very many earths.[6]

6 There are spirits whose sole study is to acquire to themselves knowledges, because they are delighted only with knowledges. Therefore these spirits are permitted to wander about, and even to pass out of this solar system into others, and to procure for themselves knowledges. They have declared that there are earths inhabited by men, not only in this solar system, but also out of it in the starry heaven, to an immense number. These spirits are from the planet Mercury.

7 As to what in general concerns the Divine worship of the inhabitants of other earths, those of them who are not idolaters, all acknowledge the Lord as the only God; for they adore the Divine not as invisible, but as visible, also for this reason, because when the Divine appears to them, He appears in the human form, as He also formerly appeared to Abraham and others on this earth;[7] and they who adore the Divine under a human form, are all accepted by the Lord.[8] They say also, that no one can rightly worship God, much less be joined to Him, unless He comprehends Him by some idea, and that God cannot be comprehended except in the human form; and if He be not so comprehended, the interior sight, which is of the thought, concerning God, is dissipated, as the sight of the eye when looking upon the boundless universe; and that in this case the thought cannot but sink into nature, and worship nature as God.

8 Then they were told that the Lord on our earth assumed the Human, they mused awhile, and presently said, that it was done for the salvation of the human race.

---

[6] Heaven corresponds to the Lord, and man as to each and all things corresponds to heaven, and hence heaven, before the Lord, is a man in a large effigy, and may be called the Greatest Man (n. 2996, 2998, 3624-3649, 3636-3643, 3741-3745, 4625) Concerning the correspondence of man, and of all things pertaining to him, with the Greatest Man, which is heaven, in general, from experience (n. 3021, 3624-3649, 3741-3751, 3883-3896, 4039-4051, 4215-4228, 4318-4331, 4403-4421, 4527-4533, 4622-4633, 4652-4660, 4791-4805, 4931-4953, 5050-5061, 5171-5189, 5377-5396, 5552-5573, 5711-5727, 10,030).

[7] The inhabitants of all the earths adore the Divine under a human form, consequently the Lord (n. 8541-8547, 10, 159, 10, 736-10, 738). And they rejoice when they hear that God actually became Man (n. 9361). It is impossible to think of God except in a human form (n. 8705, 9359, 9972). Man can worship and love what he has some idea of, but not what he has no idea of (n. 4733, 5110, 5633, 7211, 9267, 10067).

[8] The Lord receives all who are in good and who adore the Divine under a human form (n. 9359, 7173).

TWO

The Planet Mercury

9 THAT THE WHOLE HEAVEN RESEMBLES ONE MAN, WHICH IS therefore called the *Greatest Man,* and that each and all things with man, both his exteriors and interiors, correspond to that man or heaven, is an arcanum not yet known in the world; but that it is so, has been abundantly shown. To constitute that Greatest Man, there is need of spirits from many earths, those who come from our earth into heaven not being sufficient for this purpose, being respectively few; and it is provided by the Lord, that whenever there is a deficiency in any place as to the quality or quantity of correspondence, immediately those are summoned from another earth who can fill up the deficiency, that the proportion may be preserved, and thus heaven be kept in due consistence.

10 It was also disclosed to me from heaven, in what relation to the Greatest Man the spirits from the planet Mercury stand, namely, that they have relation to the memory, but to the memory of things abstracted from terrestrial and merely material objects. Since however it has been granted to speak with them, and this during many weeks, and to learn their nature and quality, and to explore how the inhabitants of that earth are particularly circumstanced, I will adduce the experiences themselves.

11 Some spirits came to me, and it was declared from heaven, that they were from the earth which is nearest to the sun, and which in our earth is called by the name of the planet Mercury. Immediately on their coming, they sought from my memory what I knew. Spirits can do this most dexterously, for when they come to man, they see in his memory all things contained therein.[1] During their search for various things, and amongst others, for the cities and places where I had been, I observed that they did not wish to know anything of temples, palaces, houses, or streets, but only of those things which I knew were transacted in those places, also of whatever related to the government therein, and to the genius and manners of the inhabitants, and similar things: for such things cohere with places in man's memory; wherefore when the places are recalled, those things also are brought up. I wondered that they were of such a nature; wherefore I asked them, why they disregarded the magnificence of the places, and only attended to the things and deeds done there. They said they had no delight in looking at things material, corporeal, and terrestrial, but only at things real. Hence it was confirmed, that the spirits of that earth, in the Greatest Man, have relation to the memory of things abstracted from what is material and terrestrial.

12 It was told me, that such is the life of the inhabitants of that earth, namely, that they have no concern about things terrestrial and corporeal, but only about the statutes, laws, and forms of government, of the nations therein; also about the things of heaven, which are innumerable. And I was further informed, that many of the men of that earth speak with spirits, and that thence they have the knowledges of spiritual things, and of the states of life after death; and thence also their contempt of things corporeal and terrestrial. For they who know of a certainty, and believe in the life after death, are concerned about heavenly things, as being eternal and happy, but not about worldly things, only so far as the necessities of life require. Because the inhabitants of Mercury are such, therefore also the spirits who are from thence are of a like nature.

---

[1] Spirits enter into all the things of man's memory but not from their own memory into man's (n. 2488, 5863, 6192, 6193, 6198, 6199, 6214). Angels enter into the affections and ends, from which and for the sake of which man thinks, wills, and acts in such and such a manner and not otherwise (n. 1317, 1645, 5844).

13 With what eagerness they inquire into and imbibe the knowledges of things, such as appertain to the memory elevated above the sensual things of the body, was made manifest to me from this, that when they looked into those things which I knew respecting heavenly things, they passed hastily through them all, and continually saying that this and that were so and so. For when spirits come to man, they enter into all his memory, and excite thence whatever suits themselves: yea, what I have often observed, they read the things contained therein, as out of a book.[2] These spirits did this with greater dexterity and expedition, because they did not stop at such things as are heavy and sluggish, and which confine and consequently retard the internal sight, as all terrestrial and corporeal things do, when regarded as ends, that is, when alone loved: but they looked into things themselves; for such things, which are not clogged with things terrestrial, carry the mind upwards, thus into a broad field; whereas mere material things carry the mind downwards, and at the same time limit and shut it up. Their eagerness to acquire knowledges, and to enrich the memory, was manifest also from the following experience. Once while I was writing something concerning things to come, and they were at a distance, so that they could not look into those things from my memory, because I was not willing to read them in their presence, they were very indignant, and contrary to their usual behavior, they were desirous to inveigh against me, saying that I was one of the worst of men, and the like; and that they might give proof of their resentment, they caused a kind of contraction attended with pain on the right side of my head even to the ear. But these things did not hurt me. Nevertheless, in consequence of having done evil, they removed themselves to a yet greater distance, but presently they stood still again, desirous to know what I had written; such is their eager thirst after knowledges.

14 The spirits of Mercury, above all other spirits, possess the knowledges of things, as well respecting this solar system, as respecting the earths which are in the starry heavens; and what they have once acquired to themselves, that they retain, and also recollect as

---

[2] That the spirits who are with man, are in possession of all things appertaining to his memory (n.5853, 5857, 5859, 5860).

often as anything similar occurs. Hence also it may appear manifest, that spirits have memory, and that it is much more perfect than the memory of men; and further, that what they hear, see, and apperceive, they retain, and especially such things as delight them, as these spirits are delighted with the knowledges of things. For whatever things cause delight, and affect the love, these flow in as it were spontaneously, and remain; other things do not enter, but only touch the surface and pass by.

15 When the spirits of Mercury come to other societies, they explore and collect from them what they know, and then they depart; for such communication is granted amongst spirits and especially amongst angels, that when they are in a society, if they are accepted and loved, all things which they know are communicated.[3]

16 In consequence of their knowledges, the spirits of Mercury are more proud than others; wherefore they were told, that although they knew innumerable things, yet there are infinite things which they do not know; and that if their knowledges should increase to eternity, the notice even of all general things would still be unattainable. They were told likewise of their pride and elation of mind, and that this is unseemly; but they replied, that it is not pride, but only a glorying by reason of the faculty of their memory; thus they were able to excuse their faults.

17 They are averse to vocal speech, because it is material; wherefore when I conversed with them without intermediate spirits, I could only do it by a species of active thought. Their memory, as consisting of things not of images purely material, supplies objects that are nearer to the thought; for the thought, which is above the imagination, requires for its objects things abstracted from material. But notwithstanding this, the spirits of Mercury are little distinguished for their judgment, having no delight in the exercise of that faculty, and the deducing of conclusions from knowledges; for bare knowledges alone are delightful to them.

---

[3] That in the heavens there is given a communication of all goods, inasmuch as it is the property of heavenly love to communicate all its possessions with others; and that hence the angels derive wisdom and happiness (n. 549, 550, 1390, 1391, 1399, 10,130, 10,723).

18 They were asked whether they wished to make any use of their knowledges; for it is not enough to be delighted with knowledges, because knowledges have respect to uses, and uses ought to be the ends of knowledges; from knowledges alone no use results to them, but to others with whom they are disposed to communicate their knowledges; and that it is very inexpedient for any one who wishes to be wise, to rest satisfied with mere knowledges, these being only administering causes, intended to be subservient to the investigation of things appertaining to life: but they replied, that they were delighted with knowledges, and that knowledges to them are uses.

19 Some of them are also unwilling to appear as men, like the spirits of other earths, and would rather appear as crystalline globes. The reason why they are desirous to appear so, although they do not so appear, is because the knowledges of things immaterial are represented in the other life by crystals.

20 The spirits of Mercury differ altogether from the spirits of our earth, for the spirits of our earth do not care so much about realities, but about worldly, corporeal, and terrestrial things, which are material; wherefore the spirits of Mercury cannot be together with the spirits of our earth, therefore wheresoever they happen to meet them, they flee away; for the spiritual spheres, which are exhaled from each, are almost contrary. The spirits of Mercury have a common saying, that they do not wish to look at a sheath, but at things stripped of their sheath, that is, at interior things.

21 There appeared a whitish flame, burning briskly, and this for nearly an hour. That flame signified the approach of spirits of Mercury, who for penetration, thought, and speech, were more prompt than the former spirits. When they were come, they instantly ran through the things contained in my memory, but I could not perceive what they observed by reason of their promptitude. I heard them afterwards saying that such is the case; in respect to what I had seen in the heavens and in the world of spirits, they said that they knew those things before. I perceived that a multitude of spirits consociated with them was behind, a little to the left in the plane of the occiput.

22 At another time I saw a multitude of such spirits, but at some distance from me, in front a little to the right, and thence they discoursed with me, but through intermediate spirits; for their speech was as quick as thought, which does not fall into human speech, but by means of other spirits. And what surprised me, they spake in a volume, and yet readily and rapidly. Their speech was perceived as undulatory, because of many together, and what is remarkable, it was conveyed towards my left eye, although they were to the right. The reason was, because the left eye corresponds to the knowledges of things abstracted from what is material, consequently to such things as appertain to intelligence: whereas the right eye corresponds to such things as appertain to wisdom.[4] They likewise perceived and judged of what they heard with the same promptitude with which they discoursed, saying of such a thing that it was so, and of such a thing that it was not so; their judgment was as it were instantaneous.

23 There was a spirit from another earth, who could speak dexterously with them, because he spoke promptly and quickly, but who affected elegance in his discourse. They instantly decided on whatever he spoke, saying of this, that it was too elegant; of that, that it was too polished: so that the sole thing they attended to was, whether they could hear anything from him which they had never known before, rejecting thus the things which caused obscurity, which are especially affectations of elegance of discourse and erudition; for these bide real things, and instead thereof present expressions, which are only material forms of things; for the speaker keeps the attention fixed herein, and is desirous that his expressions should be regarded more than the meaning of them, whereby the ears are more affected than the mind.

24 The spirits of the earth Mercury do not abide long in one place, or within companies of the spirits of one world, but wander through the universe. The reason is, because they have relation to the memory of things, which memory must be continually enriched.

---

[4] The eye corresponds to the understanding, because the understanding is the internal sight, and the sight of things immaterial (n. 2701, 4410, 4526, 9051, 10,569). The sight of the left eye corresponds to truths, consequently to intelligence; and the sight of the right eye corresponds to the goods of truth, consequently to wisdom (n. 4410). * A more accurate translation would be "in a rolling fashion."

Hence it is granted them to wander about, and to acquire to themselves knowledges in every place. During their sojourning in this manner, if they meet with spirits who love material things, that is, things corporeal and terrestrial, they avoid them, and betake themselves where they do not hear such things. Hence it may appear, that their mind is elevated above things of sense, and thus that they are in interior light. This was also given me actually to perceive, whilst they were near me, and discoursed with me: I observed at such times, that I was withdrawn from things of sense, insomuch that the light of my eyes began to grow dull and obscure.

25 The spirits of that earth go in companies and phalanxes, and when assembled together, they form as it were a globe. Thus they are joined together by the Lord, that they may act in unity, and that the knowledges of each may be communicated with all, and the knowledges of all with each, as is the case in heaven.[5] That they wander through the universe to acquire the knowledges of things, appeared to me also from this, that once, when they appeared very far from me, they discoursed with me thence, and said, that they were then gathered together, and journeying out of the sphere of this world into the starry heaven, where they knew such spirits existed as had no concern about terrestrial and corporeal things, but only about things elevated above them, with whom they wished to be. It was said, that they themselves do not know whither they are going, but that they are led from the Divine auspices to those places where they may be instructed concerning such things as they do not yet know, and which agree with the knowledges that they have already. It was also said, that they do not know how to find the companions with whom they are joined together, and that this also is done from the Divine auspices.

26 Because of their thus journeying through the universe, and thereby being enabled to know more than others respecting the worlds and earths out of the sphere of our solar system, I have also spoken with them on this subject. They said that in the universe there

---

[5] That in the heavens there is given a communication of all goods, inasmuch as it is the property of heavenly love to communicate all its possessions with others; and that hence the angels derive wisdom and happiness (n. 549, 550, 1390, 1391, 1399, 10,130, 10,723).

are very many earths inhabited by men; and that they wonder how any should suppose, whom they called men of little judgment, that the heaven of the omnipotent God consisted only of spirits and angels who come from one earth, when these comparatively are so few that in respect to the omnipotence of God they are scarce anything, even if there should he myriads of worlds, and myriads of earths. They said, moreover, that they knew there were earths existing in the universe to the number of some hundred thousands and upwards; and yet what is this to the Divine, which is infinite?

27 The spirits of Mercury, who were with me whilst I was writing and explaining the Word as to its internal sense, and who perceived what I wrote: said that the things which I wrote were in a manner gross, and that almost all the expressions appeared as material; but it was given to reply, that to the men of our earth what was written seemed subtle and elevated, and many things incomprehensible. I added, that many on this earth do not know that it is the internal man which acts into the external, and causes the external to live; and that they persuade themselves from the fallacies of the senses that the body has life, and that in consequence thereof, such as are evil and unbelieving entertain doubt respecting the life after death; also, that the part of man which is to live after death is not by them called spirit, but soul; and that they dispute what soul is, and where is its abode, and believe that the material body, although dispersed to all the winds, is to be joined again to it, in order that man may live as man; with many other things of a like nature. The spirits of Mercury, on hearing these things, asked, whether such men could become angels; and it was given to answer, that those become angels who have lived in the good of faith and charity, and that then they are no longer in external and material things, but in internal and spiritual; and then they come into that state, that they are in a light superior to that in which the spirits from mercury are. That they might know that it was so, an angel was allowed to discourse with them, who had come into heaven from our earth, who had been such when he lived in the world, concerning whom more will be said presently.

28 Afterwards there was sent me by the spirits of Mercury a long piece of paper, of an irregular shape, consisting of several pieces pasted together, which appeared as if printed with types, as on this earth. I asked whether they had the art of printing amongst them; but they said they had not, nevertheless they knew that on our earth we had such printed papers. They did not wish to say more; but I perceived that they thought that knowledges in our earth were upon paper, and not so much in man, thus insinuating that the papers knew what man did not. But they were instructed how this really is. After some time they returned, and sent me another paper, which appeared also printed like the former, but not so pasted together and irregular, but neat and handsome. They said, that they were further informed, that in our earth there are such papers, and books made of them.

29 From what has now been said, it appears manifest, that spirits retain in the memory what they see and hear in the other life, and that they are capable of being instructed alike as when they were men in the world, consequently of being instructed in the things of faith, and thereby of being perfected. The more interior spirits and angels are, in the same proportion they receive instruction more readily, and in a greater fullness, and retain it more perfectly: and inasmuch as this faculty abides forever, it is evident that they are continually increasing in wisdom. With the spirits of Mercury there is a constant growth in the science of things, but not in wisdom thence derived, because they love knowledges, which are means, but not uses which are ends.

30 The genius of the spirits who are from the planet Mercury, may still further appear from the following account. It is to be known, that all spirits and angels whatsoever, were once men for the human race is the seminary of heaven; also that the spirits are altogether such, as to affections and inclinations, as they were during their life in the world whilst men; for every one's life follows him.[6] This being the case, the genius of the men of every earth may be known from the genius of the spirits who are thence.

31 Inasmuch as the spirits of Mercury in the Greatest Man have relation to the memory of things abstracted from what is material,

---

[6] Every one's life remains with him and follows him after death (n. 4227, 7440). The externals of life are kept closed after death, and the internals opened (n. 4314, 5128, 6495). Then all and each of the things of thought are made manifest (n. 4633, 5128).

therefore when any one discourses with them concerning things terrestrial, corporeal, and merely worldly, they are altogether unwilling to hear him; and if they are forced to hear, they transmute the things spoken of into other things, and for the most part into things contrary, that they may avoid them.

32 That I might know for certain, that such is their genius, it was allowed to represent to them meadows, fallow lands, gardens, woods, and rivers; to represent such things is imaginatively to exhibit them before another, in which case, in another world, they appear to the life; but they instantly transmuted them, obscuring the meadows and fallow fields, and by representations filling them with snakes. The rivers they made black, so that the water no longer appeared limpid. When I asked them why they did so, they said that they did not wish to think of such things, but of things real, which are the knowledges of things abstracted from what is terrestrial, especially of such things as exist in the heavens.

33 Afterwards I represented to them birds of different sizes, both large and small, such as exist on our earth; for in the other life such things may be represented to the life. When they saw the birds represented, they at first wished to change them, but afterwards they were delighted with them and were satisfied. The reason was, because birds signify the knowledges of things, and the perception of this then flowed in also.[7] Thus they desisted from transmuting them, and thereby from averting the ideas of their memory. Afterwards it was allowed to represent before them a most pleasant garden full of lamps and lights; then they paused, and their attention was fixed, for the reason that lamps with lights signify truths which shine from good.[8] Hence it was made manifest that their attention might be fixed in viewing things material, if only the signification of those things in the spiritual sense was insinuated at the same time; for the things of the spiritual sense are not so abstracted from things material, since these are representatives of them.

---

[7] Birds signify things rational, intellectual, thoughts, ideas, and knowledges (n. 40, 745, 776, 778, 866, 988, 993, 5149, 7441). And this with variety according to the genera and species of birds (n. 3219).

[8] Lamps with lights signify truths shining from good (n. 4638, 9548, 9783).

34 Moreover I spoke with them concerning sheep and lambs, but they were not willing to hear of such things, because they were perceived by them as things terrestrial. The reason was, because they did not understand what innocence is, which lambs signify, as was perceivable from this, that when I told them that lambs, represented in heaven, signify innocence,[9] they immediately said that they did not know what innocence was, but only knew it as to the name; and this was because they are affected only with knowledges, and not with uses, which are the ends of knowledges, consequently they cannot know from internal perception what innocence is.

35 Some of the spirits of the earth Mercury came to me, being sent by others, to bear what I was employed about. One of the spirits of our earth said to them, that they might tell those who sent them not to speak anything but what was true, and not, according to their usual practice, suggest things opposite to those who questioned them; for if any of the spirits of our earth were to do so, he would he punished. But immediately the company which was at a distance, from which those spirits were sent, made answer, that if they were to be punished on that account, they must all he punished, since by reason of acquired habit they could not do otherwise. They said that when they speak with the men of their own earth, they also do so, but this not with any intention of deceiving, but to inspire the desire of knowing; for when they suggest things opposite, and conceal things in a certain manner, then the desire of knowing is excited, and thereby from the endeavor to search out those things, the memory is perfected. I also spoke with them at another time on the same subject, and because I knew that they spoke with the men of their earth, I asked them in what manner they instruct their inhabitants. They said that they do not instruct them how the matter is, but still they insinuate some perception thereof, that thus a desire of examining and knowing may be cherished and grow; which desire would perish, in case they answered everything. They added, that they suggest things opposite also, for this reason, that the truth afterwards may better appear; for all truth is made manifest by relation to its opposites.

---

[9] Lambs in heaven, and in the Word, signify innocence (n. 3994, 7840, 10,132).

36 It is their custom not to declare to another what they know, but still they desire to learn from all others what is known to them. But with their own society they communicate all things, insomuch that what one knows all know, and what all know each one there knows.[10]

37 Because the spirits of Mercury abound in knowledges, they are in a certain kind of pride; hence they imagine that they know so much, that it is almost impossible to know more. But it was told them by the spirits of our earth, that they do not know many, but few things, and that the things which they do not know are respectively infinite, and that those things which they do not know, compared to the things they know, are like the waters of the largest ocean compared with the waters of a very small fountain; and further, that the first step to wisdom is to know, acknowledge, and perceive that what is known is little and scarce anything in comparison with what is unknown. To convince them that this is the case, it was granted, that a certain angelic spirit should speak with them, and should tell them in general what they knew, and what they did not know, and that there were infinite things which they did not know, also that to eternity they could not even know the general things. He spoke by angelic ideas much more readily than they did, and because he discovered to them what they knew, and what they did not know, they were struck with amazement. Afterwards I saw another angel speaking with them, who appeared in some altitude to the right. He was from our earth, and enumerated very many things which they did not know. Afterwards he spoke with them by changes of state, which they said they did not understand. Then he told them that every change of state contains infinite things, as did also every smallest part of such change. When they heard these things, inasmuch as they had been in pride on account of their knowledges, they began to humble themselves. Their humiliation was represented by the sinking downwards of their volume; for that company then appeared as a volume, in front at a distance towards the left, in the plane of the

---

[10] That in the heavens there is given a communication of all goods, inasmuch as it is the property of heavenly love to communicate all its possessions with others; and that hence the angels derive wisdom and happiness (n. 549, 550, 1390, 1391, 1399, 10,130, 10,723).

region below the navel, but the volume appeared as it were hollowed in the middle, and elevated on the sides; a reciprocal moving was also observed therein. They were likewise told what that signified, that is, what they thought in their humiliation, and that they who appeared elevated on the sides were not as yet in any humiliation. And I saw that the volume was separated, and that they who were not in humiliation were remanded back towards their orb, the rest remaining where they were.

38 Spirits of Mercury came to a certain spirit from our earth, who during his abode in the world had been most distinguished for his learning (it was Christian Wolf[11]), desiring to receive information from him on various subjects. But when they perceived that what he said was not elevated above the sensual things of the natural man, because in speaking his thoughts were intent on honor, and he was desirous, as in the world (for in the other life every one is like his former self), to connect various things into series, and from those series again and continually to form other conclusions, and thus from such conclusions to link together still more, which they did not see or acknowledge to be true, and which therefore they declared to be chains which neither cohered in themselves, nor with the conclusions, calling them the obscurity of authority; they then desisted from asking him further questions, inquiring only, *how this is called, and how that;* and because he answered these inquiries also by material ideas, and by no spiritual ones, they retired from him. For every one, in the other life, speaks spiritually, or by spiritual ideas, so far as he had believed in God, and materially, so far as he had not believed. An occasion here offering itself, it is permitted to mention how it is in the other life with the learned who acquire intelligence from their own meditation, kindled with the love of knowing truths, for the sake of truths, thus for the sake of uses abstracted from worldly considerations, and how with those who acquire intelligence from others, without any meditation of their own, as they are wont to do who desire to know truths solely for the sake of a reputation for learning, and thereby for honor or gain in the world; thus who desire to know truth, not for the sake of uses abstracted from worldly consid-

---

[11] Christian Wolf[f] (1679-1754) was an eminent German philosopher.

erations: concerning such, it is allowed to relate the following experience. A certain sound was perceived penetrating from beneath, near the left side even to the left ear. I observed that they were spirits, who there attempted to force a way; but of what sort they were I could not know. However, when they had forced a way, they spoke with me, saying that they were logicians and metaphysicians, and that they had immersed their thoughts in such things, with no other end than to be accounted learned, and thus to be advanced to honor and wealth, lamenting that they now led a miserable life in consequence of having acquired those sciences with no other end, and thus not having cultivated thereby their rational; their speech was slow, and of a low tone. In the meantime there were two discoursing with each other above my head, and on inquiring who they were, it was said that one of them was most renowned in the learned world, and it was given me to believe that it was Aristotle. Who the other was, was not stated. The former was then let into the state in which he was during his life in the world; for every one may easily be let into the state of his life which he had in the world, because be has with him every state of his former life. But, what surprised me, he applied himself to the right ear, and there spoke, but in a hoarse tone of voice, yet sanely. From the purport of his speech I perceived, that he was altogether of a different genius from those schoolmen who first ascended, in that he evolved from his own thought the things he had written, and thence he produced his philosophy; so that the terms which he invented, and which he imposed on subjects of thought, were forms of expression by which he described interior things; also that he was excited to such things by a delight of the affection, and by a desire of knowing the things of the thought and understanding, and that he followed obediently whatever his spirit had dictated. Therefore he applied himself to the right ear, contrary to the custom of his followers, who are called schoolmen, and who do not go from thought to terms, but from terms to thoughts, thus in a contrary way; and many of them do not even proceed to thoughts, but stick solely in terms, which if they apply, it is to confirm whatever they desire, and to impose on falsities an appearance of truth according to their cupidity of persuading. Hence philosophical things are rather means of becoming insane than means of becoming wise; and hence they have darkness instead of light. Afterwards I spoke with him concerning the science of analysis, observing that a child, in half an hour, speaks more philosophically, analytically, and logically, than he could describe by a volume, inasmuch as all things of the thought, and thence of human speech are analytical, the laws whereof are from the spiritual world; and he who desires to think artificially from terms, is not unlike a dancer, who would learn to dance by the science of the moving fibers and muscles, in which science, if he should fix his mind whilst he is dancing, it would be almost impossible for him to move a foot; and yet without that science, he moves all the moving fibers throughout the whole body, and in subordination thereto be moves the lungs, the diaphragm, the sides, the arms, the neck, and other organs of the body, to describe all which volumes would not suffice; and it is similar with those who are desirous to think from terms. He approved of these things, saying, that to learn to think in that way, is proceeding in an inverted order, adding if any one will be so foolish, let him so proceed; but let him think continually concerning use, and from what is interior. He next showed me, what idea he had conceived of the Supreme Deity, namely, that he had represented Him to himself as having a human face, and encompassed about the head with a radiant circle; and that now be knew that the Lord is Himself that Man, and that the radiant circle is the Divine from Him, which not only flows into heaven, but also into the universe, disposing and ruling all things therein. He added, Whosoever disposes and rules heaven, also disposes and rules the universe, because the one cannot be separated from the other. He also said that he believed in one God only, whose attributes and qualities were distinguished by a variety of names, and that these names were by others worshiped as gods. There appeared to me a woman, who stretched out her hand, desiring to stroke my cheek, and when I wondered at this, he said that when he was in the world such a woman had often appeared to him, as it were stroking his cheek, and that her hand was beautiful. The angelic spirits said that such women sometimes appeared to the ancients, and were by them called Pallases, and that she appeared to him from the spirits, who, during their abode on earth, in ancient times, were delighted with ideas, and indulged in thoughts, but without philosophy: and because such spirits were with him, and were delighted with him, because he thought from the interior, therefore they representatively exhibited such a woman. Lastly, he informed me what idea he had conceived of the soul or spirit of man, which he called *pneuma,* namely, that it was an invisible vital principle, like somewhat of ether; and he said that he knew that his spirit would live after death, inasmuch as it was his interior essence, which cannot die, because it is capable of thinking; and that moreover he was not able to think clearly concerning it, but only obscurely, because he had not formed any thought about it from any other source than from himself, and a little also from the ancients. Moreover Aristotle is among sound spirits in the other life, and many of his followers are among the foolish.

39 I once saw that spirits of our earth were with spirits of the earth Mercury, and I heard them discoursing together, and the spirits of our earth, amongst other things, asked them in whom they believed. They replied that they believed in God; but when they inquired further concerning the God in whom they believed, they were unwilling to say, it being customary with them not to answer questions directly. Then the spirits from the earth Mercury, in their turn, asked the spirits from our earth in whom they believed, They said that they believed in the Lord God. The spirits of Mercury then said that they perceived that they believed in no God, and that they had contracted a habit of professing with the mouth that they believe, when yet they do not believe, The spirits of Mercury have exquisite perception, in consequence of their continually exploring, by means of perception, what others know. The spirits of our earth were of the number of those who in the world had made profession of faith agreeable to the doctrine of the church, but still had not lived the life of faith; and they who do not live the life of faith, in the other life have not faith, because it is not in the man.[12] On hearing this they were silent, inasmuch as, by apperception then given them, they acknowledged that it was so.

---

[12] They who make profession of faith from doctrine and do not live the life of faith, have no faith (n. 3865, 7766, 7778, 7790, 7950, 8094). And their interiors are contrary to the truths of faith, although in the world they do not know this (n. 7790, 7950).

40 There were certain spirits who knew from heaven, that on a time a promise was made to the spirits of the earth Mercury, that they should see the Lord; wherefore they were asked by the spirits about me whether they recollected that promise. They said that they did recollect it; but that they did not know whether it had been promised in such a way as to be beyond doubt. Whilst they were thus discoursing together, the sun of heaven then appeared to them. The sun of heaven, which is the Lord, is seen only by those who are in the inmost or third heaven; others see the light thence derived. On seeing the sun, they said that this was not the Lord God, because they did not see a face. Meanwhile the spirits discoursed with each other, but I did not hear what they said. But suddenly, the sun again appeared, and in the midst of it the Lord, encompassed with a solar circle: on seeing this the spirits of Mercury humbled themselves profoundly and subsided. Then also the Lord, from that sun, appeared to the spirits of this earth, who, when they were men, saw Him in the world; and they all, one after another, and thus many in order, confessed that it was the Lord Himself. This confession they made before all the company. Then also the Lord, out of the sun, appeared to the spirits of the planet Jupiter, who declared aloud that it was He Himself whom they had seen on their earth when the God of the universe appeared to them.[13]

41 Certain of them, after the Lord appeared, were led away towards the front to the right, and as they advanced, they said that they saw a light much clearer and purer than they had ever seen before, and that it was impossible any light could exceed it; and it was then evening here. There were many who said this.[14]

---

[13] The Lord is the sun of heaven, from whom is all light there (n. 1053, 3636, 4060). And the Lord thus appears to those who are in His celestial kingdom, where love to Him reigns (n. 1521, 1529-1531, 1837, 4696). He appears at a middle distance above the plane of the right eye (n. 4321, 7078). Therefore by "sun" in the word is signified the Lord as to Divine love (n. 2495, 4060, 7083). The sun of this world does not appear to spirits and angels, but in the place thereof there appears somewhat as it were darkish, not in front, but behind and opposite to the sun of heaven, or to the Lord (n. 9755).

[14] There is in the heavens great light, which exceeds, by many degrees, the noonday light of this world (n. 1117, 1521, 1533, 1619-1632. 4527, 5400, 8644). All light in the heavens is from the Lord as a sun there (n. 1053, 1521, 3195, 3341, 3636, 3643, 4415, 9548. 9684, 10,809). The Divine truth proceeding from the Divine good of the Divine love of the Lord appears in the heavens as light, and furnishes all the light that is there (n. 3195, 3222, 5400, 8644, 9399, 9548, 9684). The light of heaven illumines both the sight and the understanding of the angels (n. 2776, 3138). When heaven is said to be in light and heat, it signifies being in wisdom and in love (n. 3643, 9399, 9401).

42 It is to be known that the sun of the world does not appear to any spirit, nor anything of light thence. The light of that sun is as dense as thick darkness to spirits and angels. That sun remains only in the perception with spirits from having seen it during their abode in the world, and is presented to them in idea as somewhat dark-ish, and this behind at a considerable distance, in an altitude a little above the plane of the head. The planets which are within the system of that sun appear according to a determinate situation in respect to the sun; Mercury behind, a little towards the right; the planet Venus to the left, a little backwards; the planet Mars to the left in front; the planet Jupiter in like manner to the left in front, but at a greater dis-tance; the planet Saturn directly in front, at a considerable distance; the Moon to the left, at a considerable height: the satellites also to the left in respect to their planet. Such is the situation of those planets in the ideas of spirits and angels; spirits also appear near their plan-ets, but out of them. As to what particularly concerns the spirits of Mercury, they do not appear in any certain quarter, or at any certain distance, but sometimes in front, sometimes to the left, sometimes a little to the back; the reason is, because they are allowed to wander through the universe to procure for themselves knowledges.

43 Once the spirits of Mercury appeared to the left in a globe, and afterwards in a volume extending itself lengthways. I wondered whither they were desirous of going, whether to this earth or else-where; and presently I observed that they inclined to the right, and as they rolled along, approached to the earth or planet Venus towards the quarter in front. But when they came thither they said they were unwilling to be there, because the inhabitants were evil; wherefore they turned about to the back part of that earth, and then said that they would willingly stay there, because the inhabitants were good. When this took place, I felt a remarkable change in the brain, and a powerful operation thence proceeding. Hence I was led to conclude that the spirits of Venus, who were on that part of the planet, were in concord with the spirits of Mercury, and that they had relation to the memory of things material which was in concord with the memory of things immaterial, to which latter memory the spirits of Mercury have relation: hence a more powerful operation was felt from them when they were there.

44 I was desirous to know what kind of face and body the men in the earth Mercury had, whether they were like the men on our earth. There was then presented before my eyes a woman exactly resembling the women in that earth. She had a beautiful face, but it was smaller than that of a woman of our earth; her body also was more slender, but her height was equal; she wore on her head a linen cap, which was put on without art, but yet in a manner becoming. A man also was presented to view, who was more slender in body than the men of our earth are. He was clad in a garment of dark blue color, closely fitted to his body, without any foldings or protuberances. It was said that such was the form of body and such the dress of the men of that earth. Afterwards there was presented to view a species of their oxen and cows, which indeed did not differ much from those on our earth, but were smaller, and in some degree approached to species of hinds and deer.

45 They were also asked about the sun of the world, how it appears from their earth. They said that it appears large, and larger there than when seen from other earths, and they said they knew this from the ideas of other spirits concerning the sun. They said further that they enjoy a middle temperature, neither too hot nor too cold. It was then granted me to tell them, that it was so provided of the Lord in regard to them that they should not be exposed to too much heat by reason of their greater nearness to the sun, inasmuch as heat does not arise from the sun's nearness, but from the altitude and density of the atmosphere, as appears from the cold on high mountains even in hot climates; also that heat is varied according to the direct or oblique incidence of the sun's rays, as is plain from the seasons of winter and summer in every region. These are the things which it was given me to know concerning the spirits and inhabitants of the earth Mercury.

THREE

The Planet Jupiter

46 IT WAS GRANTED ME TO ENJOY LONGER INTERCOURSE with the spirits and angels of the planet Jupiter, than with the spirits and angels from the rest of the planets; wherefore I am at liberty to relate more concerning the state of their life, and of the inhabitants of that planet. That those spirits were from that planet was evident from many things, and it was also declared from heaven.

47 The earth itself or planet Jupiter does not indeed appear to spirits and angels: for to the inhabitants of the spiritual world no earth is visible, but only the spirits and angels who come thence. They who are from the planet Jupiter appear in front to the left, at a considerable distance, and this constantly, see above (n. 42) there also is the planet. The spirits of every earth are near their earth, because they are from its inhabitants, for every man after death becomes a spirit, and because they are thus of a similar genius, and can be with the inhabitants, and serve them.

48 They related that in the region of the earth where they had lived while in the world, the multitude of men therein was as great as the earth could support; that the earth was fertile, and it abounded in all things; and that there they did not desire more than the necessaries of life; that they accounted nothing useful but so far as it was necessary; and that hence the multitude of men was so great. They said that the education of their children was their greatest concern, and that they loved them most tenderly.

49 They further related that they are there distinguished into nations, families, and houses, and that they all live apart with their own kindred; and that hence their intercourse is confined to relatives; likewise, that no one ever covets the goods of another; and that it never enters into their minds to desire the possessions of another, still less to obtain them fraudulently, and least of all to break in and plunder. This they consider as a crime against human nature, and regard it as horrible. When I would have told them that on this earth there are wars, depredations, and murders, they then turned away, and were unwilling to hear. It was declared to me by the angels that the most ancient people on this earth lived in like manner, namely, that they were distinguished into nations, families, and houses that all at that time were content with their own possessions; that it was a thing altogether unknown for one person to enrich himself from the goods of another, and to have dominion from self-love; and that on this account the ancient times, and especially the most ancient, were more acceptable to the Lord than succeeding times: and such being the state of the world, innocence also then reigned, and with it wisdom; every one then did what was good from good, and what was just from justice. To do what is good and just with a view to their own honor, or gain, was unknown. At the same time they spoke nothing but what was true, and this not so much from truth as from good, that is, not from the understanding separate from the will, but from the will conjoined with the understanding. Such were the ancient times; wherefore angels could then converse with men, and convey their minds, almost separate from things corporeal, into heaven, yea, lead them about, and show them the magnificent and blessed things there, and likewise communicate to them their happinesses and delights. These times were known also to the ancient writers, and were by them called the golden and also Saturnian ages. The reason that those times were such, was owing to this, that men were then distinguished into nations, nations into families, and families into houses, and every house lived apart by itself; and it then never entered into any one's mind to invade another's inheritance, and thence acquire to himself opulence and dominion. Self-love and the love of the world were then far removed; every one rejoiced in his own, and not less in his neighbor's good. But in succeeding times this scene was changed, and totally reversed, when the lust of dominion and of large possessions invaded the mind. Then mankind, for the sake of self-defense, collected themselves into kingdoms and empires; and because the laws of charity and of conscience, which were inscribed on the hearts, ceased, it became necessary to enact laws in order to restrain violence, in which honors and gains were rewards, and privation of them punishments. When the state of the world was thus changed, heaven removed itself from man, and this more and more even to this age, when it is no longer known whether there is a heaven and a hell, yea, by some it is denied. These things are said, that it may be illustrated by the parallel, what is the state of the inhabitants of the earth Jupiter, and whence they have their probity, and also their wisdom, concerning which more will be said hereafter.

50 By long conversation with the spirits of the earth Jupiter, it was made manifest to me that they were more upright than the spirits of most other earths. The manner of their approach to me, their abode with me, and their influx at that time, was inexpressibly gentle and sweet. In the other life the quality of every spirit manifests itself by an influx, which is the communication of his affection; uprightness by gentleness and sweetness; by gentleness, in that he fears to do hurt, and by sweetness, because he loves to do good. I could clearly distinguish a difference between the gentleness and the sweetness of the influx proceeding from the spirits of Jupiter and of that which proceeds from the good spirits of our earth. When any slight disagreement exists among them, they said that there appears a sort of slender bright irradiation, like that of lightning, or like the little swath encompassing glittering and wandering stars; but all disagreements among them are soon adjusted. Glittering stars, which are at the same time wandering, signify what is false; but glittering and fixed stars signify what is true; thus the former signify disagreement.[1]

51 I could distinguish the presence of the spirits of Jupiter, not only by the gentleness and sweetness of their approach and influx, but also from this, that for the most part their influx was into the face, and made it smiling and cheerful, and this continually during their presence. They said that they communicate a like cheerfulness of countenance to the inhabitants of their earth, when they come to them, being desirous thus to inspire them with tranquillity and delight of heart. That tranquillity and delight with which they inspired me filled my breast and heart very sensibly; at the same time cupidities and anxieties concerning things to come were removed, which cause unrest and undelightfulness, and excite various commotions in the mind. Hence it was evident to me what was the nature and quality of the life of the inhabitants of the earth Jupiter; for the disposition of the inhabitants of any earth may be known by the spirits who come thence, inasmuch as every one retains his own life after death, and continues to live it when he becomes a spirit. It was observed that they had a state of blessedness or happiness still more interior, which was manifest from this circumstance, that their interiors were perceived not to be closed, but open to heaven; for in proportion as the interiors are more open to heaven, in the same proportion they are the more susceptible of receiving Divine good, and with it blessedness and interior happiness. The case is altogether otherwise with those who do not live in the order of heaven: the interiors with such are closed, and the exteriors open to the world.

52 It was further shown me what sort of faces the inhabitants of the earth Jupiter had; not that the inhabitants themselves appeared to me, but that the spirits appeared with faces similar to what they had when on their earth. But before it was shown, one of their angels appeared behind a bright cloud, who gave leave; and then two faces were shown. They were like the faces of the men of our earth, fair and beautiful; sincerity and modesty beamed forth from them. During

---

[1] Stars in the word signify the knowledges of good and truth, consequently truths (n. 2495, 2849, 4697). And in the other life truths are represented by fixed stars, but falsities by wandering stars (n. 1128).

the presence of the spirits of Jupiter, the faces of the men of our earth appeared less than usual, which was owing to this, that there was an influx from those spirits of the idea which they had concerning their own faces as being larger; for they believe, during their abode in their earth, that after their decease their faces will he larger and of a round shape; and because this idea is impressed on them, it consequently remains with them, and when they become spirits they appear to themselves as having larger faces. The reason why they believe that their faces will be larger is, because they say that the face is not body, because through it they see, hear, speak, and manifest their thoughts; and whereas the mind is thus transparent through the face, they hence form an idea of the face as of the mind in form; and because they know that they will he wiser after their life in the world, therefore they believe that the form of the mind or the face will become larger. They believe also that after their decease they will perceive a fire which will communicate warmth to their faces. This belief takes its rise from hence, that the wiser amongst them know that fire in the spiritual sense signifies the love, and that love is the fire of life, and from this fire the angels have life.[2] Those of them also who have lived in heavenly love, obtain their wish, and perceive their face to grow warm; and then the interiors of their mind are kindled with love. For this reason the inhabitants of that earth also wash and cleanse their faces much, and protect them carefully from the heat of the sun. They have a covering made of the inner rind or bark of a tree, of a bluish color, which they wrap about the head and thus cover the face. Concerning the faces of the men of our earth, which they saw through my eyes,[3] they said that they were not beautiful, and that their beauty consisted in the external skin, but not in the fibers from the internal. They wondered that the faces of some were full of warts and pustules, or were otherwise deformed, saying that with them such faces were never seen. Some faces were always smil-

---

[2] Fire in the Word is love in both senses (n. 934, 4906, 5215). The sacred and heavenly fire is the Divine love, and every affection which is of that love (n. 934, 6314, 6832). Internal fire is the love of self and the world, and every concupiscence which is of these loves (n. 965, 1861, 5071, 6314, 6832, 7575, 10.747) Love is the fire of life, and life itself is actually thence (n. 4906, 5071, 6032).

[3] Spirits and angels do not see what is in this solar world, but they saw through my eyes (n. 1881).

ing, namely, those that were cheerful and merry, and those that were a little prominent about the lips.

53 The reason of the faces smiling that were prominent about the lips was, that the most of their speech is effected by the face, and especially by the region around the lips; and also because they never dissemble, that is, speak otherwise than they think. For this reason they do not constrain their face, but let it out freely. It is otherwise with those who from childhood have learned to dissemble. Their face is thus contracted interiorly, lest something of their thought should shine forth. Neither is it let forth outwardly, but is held ready to let itself out or contract itself, according as cunning suggests. The truth of this may be evident from an examination of the fibers of the lips and the parts around them. For there are manifold series of fibers there, folded together and intertwined, which were created not only for masticating and for speech by words, but also for expressing the ideas of the mind.

54 It was also shown how the thoughts are presented by the face. The affections of the love are manifested through the countenance and its changes, and the thoughts by variations as to the forms of the interiors therein; but they cannot be further described. The inhabitants of the earth Jupiter have also a vocal speech, but not as sonorous as ours. The one speech assists the other, and their vocal speech is inspired with life by the speech of the face. I was informed by angels that the first speech of all men on every earth was speech by the face, and this from two sources, the lips and the eyes. The reason why such speech was the first, is, that the face was formed for portraying what man thinks and wills, and thence also the face was called the image and index of the mind; also because in the most ancient or earliest times there was sincerity, and man neither thought nor wished to think anything else than what he was willing should shine forth from his face. Thus also the affections of the mind, and the thoughts therefrom, could be presented to the life, and fully. Thus also they were made apparent to the eye, very many, as it were, in a form together. This speech, therefore, as much surpassed vocal speech as sight excels hearing, or as seeing a landscape excels hearing of it, or apprehending it by verbal description. They added that such speech agrees with the speech of angels, with whom also men in those times were in communication; and further that when the face speaks, or the mind through the face, it is the angelic speech with man in ultimate natural form, but not when the mouth speaks by words. Every one, too, can comprehend that the most ancient people could not have the speech of words; since the words of language were not immediately infused into men, but had to be invented, and applied to things; which could be done only in process of time.[4] As long as sincerity and rectitude remained with man, so long also such speech remained. But as soon as the mind began to think one thing and speak another, which took place when man began to love himself and not his neighbor, then vocal speech began to develop, the face being silent or dissembling. Thus the internal form of the face was changed, contracted itself, hardened, and began to be almost void of life; but the external form, inflamed by the fire of self-love, began to appear to the eyes of men as if it were alive. For that absence of life which lies underneath, does not appear to the eyes of men, but to the eyes of angels, since these see the interiors. Such are the faces of those who think one thing and speak another; for dissimulation, hypocrisy, cunning, and deceit, which are prudence at this day, induce such effects. But it is different in the other life, where it is not permitted to speak one thing and think another. Disagreement between the speech and the thought is also there clearly perceived in every word; and when it is perceived in a spirit, he is cast out of the community, and fined. Afterward he is reduced by various methods to speak as he thinks, and to think as he wills; even till he has one undivided mind; so that if he is good, he may will good and think and speak truth from good, and if he is evil, he may will evil and think and speak falsity from evil. Not before this is effected is the good spirit elevated into heaven, nor the evil spirit cast into hell; and this to the end, that there may be in hell nothing but evil and the falsity of evil, and in heaven nothing but good and the truth of good.

---

[4] The most ancient people on this earth had speech through the face and lips, by means of internal breathing (n. 607, 1118, 7361). The people on certain other earths have a similar speech (n. 4799. 7359, 8248, 10,587). Concerning the perfection and excellence of that speech (n. 7360, 10,587, 10,708).

55 I was further informed by the spirits from that earth, concerning various particulars relating to its inhabitants, as concerning their manner of walking, their food, and their habitations. With respect to their manner of walking, they do not walk erect like the inhabitants of this and of many other earths, nor do they creep like animals; but as they go along, they assist themselves with their hands, and alternately half elevate themselves on their feet, and also at every third step turn the face sideways and behind them, and likewise at the same time bend the body a little, which is done suddenly; for with them it is thought unbecoming to be seen by others except in the face. In walking thus they always keep the face elevated as with us, that so they may look at the heavens as well as the earth. Holding the face downwards so as to look at the earth alone, they call accursed. The most vile amongst them do so, but if they continue and do not elevate the face, they are banished from the society. When they sit, they appear like men of our earth, erect as to the upper part of the body, but they usually sit cross-legged. They take special care, not only when they walk, but also when they sit, to be seen in the face, and not at the back. They are also very willing to have their faces seen, because thence their mind appears; for with them the face is never at variance with the mind, nor indeed can they make it so. Those present also know clearly from this what dispositions they entertain towards them, especially whether their apparent friendship is sincere or forced, for this they never conceal. These particulars were shown to me by their spirits, and confirmed by their angels. Hence also their spirits are seen to walk, not erect like others, but almost like persons swimming, appearing to help themselves forward with their hands, and by turns to look around them.

56 They who live in their warm climates go naked, except with a covering about the loins; nor are they ashamed of their nakedness, for their minds are chaste, and they love their consorts only, and abhor adultery. They wondered exceedingly that the spirits of our earth, who on hearing of their method of walking, and also that they were naked, ridiculed it, and had lascivious thoughts, without attending at all to their heavenly life, but only to such things. They said that this was a sign that things corporeal and terrestrial were of more

concern to them than heavenly things, and that things of an indecent
nature had place in their minds. Those spirits of our earth were told
that nakedness gives no occasion either of shame or of scandal to
such as live in chastity and a state of innocence, but only to such as
live in lasciviousness and immodesty.

57 When the inhabitants of that earth lie in bed, they turn their
faces forward, or towards the chamber, but not backward, or towards
the wall. This was told me by their spirits, who said the reason is,
that they believe that in turning the face forward they turn it to the
Lord, but if they turn it backward they avert it from the Lord. I have
sometimes observed, in regard to myself, whilst I was in bed, such a
direction of the face; but never knew before whence it was.

58 They take delight in making long meals; but not so much
from enjoyment of the food, as from enjoyment of the conversation at
that time. When they sit at table they do not sit on chairs or benches,
or raised couches of turf, nor on the grass, but on the leaves of a certain tree. They were not willing to tell of what tree the leaves were;
but when I named several by conjecture, they assented at last on my
naming the leaves of the fig-tree. They said moreover, that they do not
prepare food with reference to the taste, but especially with reference
to the use; and they added that to them useful food was savory. On
this subject a conversation arose among the spirits, and it was said
that this is the right way for man; for thus it is in his heart to have a
sound mind in a sound body, but it is otherwise with those whose
taste governs, and whose body therefore sickens, or at least inwardly
languishes, and consequently their mind also; for the action of this
depends upon the interior state of the recipient parts of the body, as
the sight and hearing upon the state of the eye and ear. Thus is seen
the insanity of placing all the delight of life in luxury and pleasure.
From this too, comes dullness in such things as are of thought and
judgment, and shrewdness in such things as are of the body and the
world. From this arises the likeness between a man and a brute ani-
mal, with which also such persons not inaptly compare themselves.

59 Their habitations were also shown me. They are low and of
wood, but within they are lined with the bark or rind of a tree of a

palish blue color, the walls and ceiling being spotted as with small stars, to represent the heavens; for they are fond of thus picturing the visible heavens and stars in the insides of their houses, because they believe the stars to be the abodes of angels. They have also tents, which are round above, and stretched out to a considerable length, spotted likewise within with little stars in a blue plane; in these they betake themselves in the middle of the day, lest their faces be injured from the heat of the sun. They take great care in the construction and in the cleanliness of these their tents. They have also their meals in them.

60 When the spirits of Jupiter saw the horses of this earth, the horses appeared to me smaller than usual, although they were tolerably robust and large. This was in consequence of the idea of those spirits concerning the horses there. They said that they also had horses with them, and much larger, but that they were wild, or in the woods, and that when they are seen, the inhabitants are terrified, although they do no harm. They added, that the fear of horses is innate or natural to them. This led me to a consideration of the cause of that fear; for "a horse" in the spiritual sense signifies the intellectual faculty formed of scientifics,[5] and because the inhabitants of Jupiter are afraid of cultivating the intellectual faculty by worldly sciences, hence comes an influx of fear. That they do not care for scientifics, which are of human erudition, will be seen in what follows.

61 The spirits of that earth are not willing to associate with the spirits of our earth, because they differ both in minds and manners. They say that the spirits of our earth are cunning, and that they are prompt and ingenious in the contrivance of evil; and that they know and think little about what is good. Moreover, the spirits of the earth Jupiter are much wiser than the spirits of our earth. They say also of our spirits, that they talk much and think little, and thus that they are not capable of an interior perception of many things, not even of what is good; hence they conclude, that the men of our earth are external men. Once also it was permitted evil spirits of our earth, by

---

[5] A "horse" signifies the intellectual faculty (n. 2760-2762, 3217, 5321, 6125, 6400, 6534, 7024, 8146, 8148). And that "the white horse" in the *Apocalypse* signifies the understanding of the Word (n. 2760).

their evil arts, to act upon and infest the spirits of Jupiter who were with me. The spirits of Jupiter endured them for a long time, but at length confessed that they could endure no longer, and that they believed it impossible for worse spirits to exist, for they perverted their imagination and also their thoughts in such a manner that they seemed to themselves as it were bound, and that they could not be extricated and set at liberty without Divine aid. Whilst I was reading in the Word some passages concerning our Savior's passion, then European spirits infused dreadful scandals, with intent to seduce the spirits of Jupiter. Inquiry was made who they were, and what had been their profession in the world, and it was discovered that some of them had been preachers; and that the greater part were of those who call themselves of the Lord's society, or Jesuits. I said that when they lived in the world, by their preaching concerning the Lord's passion, they were able to move the common people to tears. I added also the reason, that in the world they thought one way and spoke another, thus entertained one thing in the heart and professed another with the mouth; but now it was not permitted them to speak thus deceitfully, because when they become spirits, they are compelled to speak just as they think. The spirits of Jupiter were greatly astonished that there could be given such a disagreement between a man's interiors and his exteriors, so that he could speak altogether differently from what he thought; which to them was impossible. They wondered when they heard that many who are from our earth also become angels, and are of an altogether different heart, supposing at the time that all on our earth were like those present. But it was said that there are many of a different nature, and that there are also those who think from good, and not as these from evil; and that they who think from good become angels. That they might know that it was so, there came out of heaven choirs of angels from our earth, one after another, which with one voice and in harmony together glorified the Lord.[6] Those choirs so greatly delighted the spirits of Jupiter who were with me, that they seemed to themselves, as if they were caught up into heaven. The glorification by the choirs lasted about

---

[6] When many spirits speak together and unanimously they form what is called a choir, and concerning them (n. 2595, 2596, 3350). In their speech there is harmony (n. 1648, 1649). By choirs in the other life introduction into unanimity is effected (n. 5182)

an hour, and the delight they received was communicated to me and given me to feel. They said that they would tell their people about it who were elsewhere.

62. The inhabitants of the earth Jupiter place wisdom in thinking well and justly of all things that happen in life. This wisdom they derive from their parents from infancy, and it is successively transmitted to posterity, and increases from the love they have for it because of its belonging to their parents. Of sciences, such as are in our earth, they know nothing whatever, nor do they wish to know. They call them shades and compare them to clouds which hide the sun. This idea concerning the sciences they have conceived from some spirits from our earth who boasted that they were wise from sciences. The spirits from our earth who thus boasted were such as made wisdom to consist in things appertaining merely to the memory, as in languages, especially the Hebrew, Greek, and Latin, in a knowledge of the things related in the literary world, in criticism, in mere experiments, and in terms, particularly such as are philosophical, with other things of a like nature, not using such things as means leading to wisdom, but making wisdom to consist in those things themselves. Such persons, because they have not cultivated their rational faculty by the sciences, as by means leading to wisdom, have little perception in the other life; for they see only in terms, and from terms, in which case those things are as clods and clouds obstructing the intellectual sight (see above, n. 38); and they who have been proud of their erudition therefrom, have still less perception; but they who have used the sciences as means of invalidating and annihilating the things appertaining to the church and to faith, have totally destroyed their intellectual faculty, and like owls they see in the thick darkness falsity for truth, and evil for good. The spirits of Jupiter, from the conversation they had with such, concluded that sciences induce shade and blindness. But they were informed that on our earth the sciences are means of opening the intellectual sight, which sight is in the light of heaven; but because such things as appertain to the mere natural and sensual life reign, therefore the sciences to the men of our earth are means of becoming insane, namely, of confirming them in favor of nature against the Divine, and in favor of the world, against heaven. They were further informed that the sciences in themselves are spiritual riches, and that they who possess them are like those who possess worldly riches, which in like manner are means of performing uses to himself, his neighbor, and his country, and also means of doing evil. Moreover, that they are like garments, which serve for use and ornament, and also for pride, as with those who would be honored for these alone. The spirits of the earth Jupiter understood these things well; but they wondered that, being men, they should rest in means, and prefer things leading to wisdom before wisdom itself; and that they should not see, that to immerse the mind in such things, and not to elevate it above them, was to becloud and blind it.

63 A certain spirit ascending from the lower earth, came to me, and said that he had heard what I had been discoursing upon with other spirits, but that he did not understand at all what was said concerning spiritual life and the light thereof. He was asked whether he was willing to be instructed concerning it. He said that he had not come with that purpose. From which I concluded that he would not comprehend such things. He was very stupid; yet it was declared by the angels, that when he lived as a man in the world, he was much celebrated for his learning. He was cold, as was manifestly felt from his breathing, which was a sign of light merely natural, and of none spiritual, thus that by the sciences he had not opened, but had closed for himself the way to the light of heaven.

64 Because the inhabitants of the earth Jupiter procure intelligence for themselves by a way different from that of the inhabitants of our earth, and are moreover of a different genius from their life, therefore they cannot abide long together, but either shun them or remove them. There are spheres, which may be called spiritual spheres, which continually flow forth, yea, overflow from every spirit; they flow from the activity of the affections and consequent thoughts, thus from the life itself.[7] All consociations in the other life are regulated according to these spheres; those which agree being

---

[7] A spiritual sphere, which is the sphere of the life, flows forth and overflows from every man spirit, and angel, and encompasses them about (n. 4464, 5179, 7454). It flows forth from the life of their affections and consequent thoughts (n. 2489, 4464, 6206). In the other life consociations and also dissociations are according to spheres (n. 6206, 9606, 9607, 10,312).

joined together according to their agreement, and those which disagree being separated according to their disagreement. The spirits and angels who are from the earth Jupiter, in the *Greatest Man* have relation to the *imaginative of thought*, and consequently to an active state of the interior parts; but the spirits of our earth have relation to the various functions of the exterior parts of the body, and when these are desirous to have dominion, the activity or imaginative of thought from the interior cannot flow in: hence come the oppositions between the spheres of the life of each.

65 As to what concerns their Divine worship, it is a principal characteristic thereof, that they acknowledge our Lord as the Supreme, who rules heaven and earth, calling Him the only Lord; and because they acknowledge and worship Him during their life in the body, they hence seek Him after death and find Him; He is the same with our Lord. They were asked, whether they know that the only Lord is a Man. They replied that they all know that He is a Man, because in their world He has been seen by many as a Man; and that He instructs them concerning the truth, preserves them, and also gives eternal life to those who worship Him from good. They said further, that it is revealed to them from Him how they should live, and how they should believe; and that what is revealed is handed down from parents to children, and hence there flows forth doctrine to all the families, and thereby to the whole nation which is descended from one father. They added, that it seems to them as if they had the doctrine written on their minds, and they conclude so from this, because they perceive instantly, and acknowledge as of themselves, whether it be true or not what is said by others concerning the life of heaven with man. They do not know that their only Lord was born a man on our earth; they said that they care to know only that He is Man, and rules the universe. When I informed them that on our earth He is named Christ Jesus, and that Christ signifies Anointed or King, and Jesus, Savior, they said that they do not worship Him as a King, because royalty savors of what is worldly, but that they worship Him as the Savior. On this occasion a doubt was injected from the spirits of our earth, whether their only Lord was the same with our Lord; but they removed it by the recollection that they had seen

Him in the sun, and had acknowledged that it was He Himself whom they saw on their earth (see above, n. 40) Once also with the spirits of Jupiter who were with me, there flowed in for a moment a doubt whether their only Lord was the same with our Lord; but this doubt, which flowed in for a moment, was also in a moment dispersed. It inflowed from some spirits of our earth; and then, what surprised me, they were so ashamed for having doubted this, though but for a moment, that they requested me not to publish it, lest they should be charged with incredulity, when yet they now know it more than others. These spirits were very much affected and rejoiced when they heard it declared that the only Lord is alone Man, and that all have from Him what entitles them to be called men; but that they are only so far men as they are images of Him, that is, as far as they love Him, and love their neighbor, thus, so far as they are in good; for the good of love and faith is the image of the Lord.

66 There were with me some spirits of the earth Jupiter, while I was reading the seventeenth chapter in *John* concerning the Lord's love, and concerning His glorification; and when they heard the things that are there, holiness filled them, and they confessed that all things therein were Divine. But then some spirits of our earth, who were unbelievers, continually suggested various scandals, saying that He was born an infant, lived as a man, appeared as another man, was crucified, with other circumstances of a like nature. But the spirits of the earth Jupiter paid no attention to these suggestions. They said that their devils are such, whom they abhor; adding, that nothing celestial has any place in their minds, but only earthly things, which they called dross. That it was so, they said they had also discovered from this, that when they heard that on their earth they go naked, obscene ideas immediately occupied their thoughts, and they paid no attention to their celestial life, about which they had heard at the same time.

67 The clear perception which the spirits of Jupiter have concerning spiritual things, was made manifest to me from their manner of representing how the Lord converts depraved affections into good affections. They represented the intellectual mind as a beautiful form, and impressed upon it an activity suitable to the form answering to the life of affection. This they executed in a manner which no words can describe, and with such dexterity that they were commended by the angels. There were then present some of the learned from our earth, who had immersed the intellectual faculty in scientific terms, and had written and thought much about form, about substance, about materiality and immateriality, and the like, without applying such things to any use; these could not even comprehend that representation.

68 They are exceedingly cautious on their earth, lest any one should fall into wrong opinions concerning the only Lord; and if they observe that any begin to think wrongly concerning Him, they first admonish him, then use threats, and lastly deter by punishment. They said that they had observed, if any such wrong opinions insinuate themselves into any family, that family is taken from amongst them, not by the punishment of death inflicted by their fellows, but by being deprived of respiration, and consequently of life, by spirits, when they have first threatened them with death. For in that earth spirits speak with the inhabitants, and chastise them if they have done evil, and even if they have intended to do evil, of which we shall say more presently. Hence if they think evil concerning the only Lord, and do not repent, they are threatened with death. In this manner the worship of the Lord is preserved, who is to them there the Supreme Divine.

69 They said that they have no festival days, but that every morning at sunrise, and every evening at sunset, they perform holy worship to their only Lord in their tents; and that they also sing psalms after their manner.

70 I was further instructed, that in that earth there are also some who call themselves saints, and who command their servants, of whom they wish to have great numbers, to give them the title of lords, under threat of punishment. They likewise forbid them to adore the Lord of the universe, saying that themselves are mediating lords and that they will present their supplications to the Lord of the universe. They call the Lord of the universe, who is our Lord, not only the Lord, as the rest do, but the Supreme Lord, by reason that they call themselves also lords. The sun of the world they call the face of the supreme Lord, and believe that His abode is there, wherefore they also adore the sun. The rest of the inhabitants hold them in aversion and are unwilling to converse with them, as well because they adore the sun as because they call themselves lords, and are worshiped by their servants as mediatory gods. There was shown me by spirits the covering of their head, which was a tower-shaped cap of darkish color. In the other life such appear to the left in a certain altitude, and there sit as idols, and in the beginning are also worshiped by the servants who have attended upon them, but are afterwards held in derision by them also. What surprised me was, that their faces shine there as from a fire, which is in consequence of their having believed that they were saints; but notwithstanding this fiery appearance of their faces, they are nevertheless cold, and have an intense desire to be made warm. Hence it is evident that the fire, from which they shine, is the fire of self-love, and is fatuous. In order to make themselves warm, they seem to themselves to cut wood, and whilst they are cutting, there appears underneath the wood something of a man, whom at the same time they attempt to strike. This appearance is in consequence of their attributing to themselves merit and sanctity; for all who do so in the world, seem to themselves in the other life to cut wood, as was the case likewise with some spirits from our earth, who have been spoken of elsewhere. For the further illustration of this subject, I will here adduce this experience concerning them. "In the lower earth beneath the soles of the feet, are those who have placed merit in their good deeds and works. Many of them appear to themselves to cut wood. The place where they are is very cold, and they seem to themselves to acquire warmth by their labor. I have also spoken with them, and it was granted me to ask them whether they wished to come out of that place. They said that they had not yet merited it by their labor. But when that state has been gone through, they are taken out. They are natural, because to wish to merit salvation is not spiritual; for it comes from the proprium, not from the Lord. Moreover they also prefer themselves to others, and some of them despise others. If they do not receive greater joy than others in the other life, they are indignant against the Lord; for which reason, when they are cutting wood, there appears as it were something of the Lord under the wood. This comes from their indignation."[8]

71 It is common on that earth for spirits to speak with the inhabitants and to instruct them, and also to chastise them if they have done evil, in regard to which since many things have been related to me by their angels, I wish to repeat them in order. The reason why spirits speak with the men there, is that they think much about heaven and about the life after death, and have comparatively little solicitude about life in the world; for they know that they are to live after death, and in a state happy according to the state of their internal man, formed in the world. To speak with spirits and angels was also common on this earth in ancient times, and for the same reason, namely, because they then thought much of heaven and little of the world. But that living communication with heaven in process of time was closed, as man from internal became external, or what is the same, as he began to think much about the world and little about heaven; and still more when he no longer believed that there is a heaven or a hell, nor that man in himself is a spirit which lives after death; for at this day it is believed that the body lives from itself, and not from its spirit; wherefore unless man now believed that he will rise again with the body, he would have no belief in the resurrection.

72 As to what particularly regards the presence of spirits with the inhabitants of the earth Jupiter, there are some spirits who chastise, some who instruct, and some who rule over them. The spirits who chastise apply themselves to the left side, and incline themselves towards the back, and when they are there, they draw forth from the man's memory all that he has done and thought; for this is easy to spirits, for when they come near to a man, they come into all his memory. If they find that he has done evil, or thought evil, they reprove him, and also chastise him with pain of the joints, and of the feet or hands, or with a pain about the epigastric region. This also spirits

---

[8] The Lord alone has merit and justice (n. 9715, 9975, 9979, 9981, 9982). They who place merit in works, or wish to merit heaven by their good deeds, wish to be served in the other life, and are never content (n. 6393). They despise the neighbor, and are angry with the Lord Himself if they do not receive reward (n. 9976). What their lot is in the other life (n. 942, 1774, 1877, 2027). They are of those who appear to cut wood in the lower earth (n. 1110, 4943).

can do dexterously when permitted. When such come to a man they inspire horror with fear, and thus the man knows of their approach. Evil spirits can inspire fear when they approach any one, especially those who while they lived in the world were robbers. That I might know how these spirits act when they come to a man of their earth, it was permitted that such a spirit should also come to me. When he was near, horror with fear manifestly took possession of me; yet the horror was not interior but exterior, because I knew that it was such a spirit. He was also seen, and appeared like a dark cloud, with moving stars in the cloud. Moving stars signify falsities, but fixed stars truths. He applied himself to my left side toward the back, and also began to reprove me for the deeds and thoughts which he drew forth out of my memory, and also interpreted perversely; but he was prevented by angels. When he perceived that he was with one who was not a man of his earth, he began to speak with me, saying that when he came to a man, he knew each and all things that the man had done and thought; and that he reproved him severely, and also chastised him with various pains. Again at another time such a chastising spirit came to me, and applied himself to my left side below the middle of the body, like the former one, who also wished to punish me; but he too was prevented by angels. He, however, showed me the binds of punishments which they are permitted to inflict upon the men of their earth, if they do and intend to do evil. They were, besides pain of the joints, a painful constriction also around the middle of the belly, which is felt as a compression by a sharp girdle. And then there was a taking away of the breath at intervals even to distress; and also the prohibition from eating anything but bread for a time; last of all the threat of death, if they should not leave off doing such things; and also privation from enjoyment of the consort, children, and companions. Pain therefrom is also then insinuated.

73 But the spirits who instruct, also, apply themselves to the left side, but more toward the front. They also rebuke, but mildly, and presently teach them how they ought to live. They appear dark also, yet not as the former like clouds, but as if clothed in sackcloth. These are called instructors, but the former chastisers. When these spirits are present, angelic spirits are also present, sitting at the head and filling it in a peculiar manner. Their presence is also perceived there as a gentle breathing; for they fear lest from their drawing near and their influx the man should perceive the least pain or anxiety. They rule the chastising and instructing spirits; preventing the former from doing worse to the man than is permitted by the Lord, and requiring the latter to tell the truth. When the chastising spirit was with me, the angelic spirits also were then present, and kept my face continually cheerful and smiling, and the region around the lips prominent, and my mouth a little open. This the angels do easily by influx, when permitted by the Lord. They said that they induce such a countenance upon the inhabitants of their earth, when they are present.

74 If a man after chastisement and instruction again does evil, or thinks to do evil, and does not restrain himself by the precepts of truth, then, when the chastising spirit returns, he is punished more severely. But the angelic spirits moderate the punishment according to the intention in the deeds, and according to the will in the thoughts. From this it may be evident that their angels who sit at the head, have a kind of judicial authority over the man; since they permit, moderate, restrain, and flow in. But it was said that they do not judge, for the Lord alone is the Judge; and all the things which they command to the chastising and instructing spirits flow in with them from Him, though it appears as if from them.

75 Spirits there speak with man, but not man in turn with the spirits, except these words when he is instructed *that he will do so no more.* Nor is it permitted him to tell any one that a spirit has spoken with him: if one does this, he is afterward punished. Those spirits of Jupiter, when they were with me, thought at first that they were with a man of their earth; but when I spoke in turn with them, and they saw that I thought of publishing these things, and thus of telling others, and it was not then permitted them to chastise or instruct me, they perceived that they were with another.

76 There are two signs that appear to those spirits when they are with a man. They see an old man with a pale face, which is a sign that they should say nothing but what is true, and do nothing but what is just. They also see a face in a window, which is a sign that they should depart thence. That old man was also seen by me, and likewise the face in the window was seen; on seeing which the spirits immediately departed from me.

77 Besides the spirits who have now been mentioned, there are also spirits who persuade the contrary. They are those who while they lived in the world, were banished from the society of others, because they were evil. When they approach, there appears as it were a flying fire, that glides down near the face. They place themselves low down behind the man, and speak thence toward the upper parts. They speak things contrary to what the instructing spirit has said from the angels, namely, that one should not live according to the instruction, but of his own will and license, and similar things. They come for the most part after the former spirits have gone away, but the men there know who and what these spirits are, and therefore care nothing for them; yet they learn in this way what evil is, and so what good is; for by evil it is learned what good is, since the quality of good is known from its opposite. All perception of a thing is according to reflection in regard to its distinctions from things contrary, in various ways and various degrees.

78 The chastising and instructing spirits do not go to those who call themselves saints and mediating lords of whom above (n. 70), as they do to others on that earth, because these do not suffer themselves to be instructed, nor are they amended by discipline. They are inflexible, because they do this from the love of self. The spirits said that they recognize them from their coldness, and when they perceive the cold, they depart from them.

79 There are also spirits among those of Jupiter, whom they call chimney-sweepers, because they appear in such garments, and also with a sooty face. Who and what they are, I am also permitted to describe. One such spirit came to me, and earnestly begged me to intercede for him that he might come into heaven. He said that he did not know that he had done evil, only that he had reproved the inhabitants of that earth; adding that after he had reproved, he instructed them. He applied himself to my left side under the elbow, and spoke as with a cracked voice; he could also move to pity. But I

could only reply that I could bring him no help, and that this is of the Lord alone; and that I could not intercede, because I did not know whether it would be useful or not, but if he was worthy he might have hope. He was then sent back among the upright spirits from his earth; but they said that he could not be in their company, because he was not such as they. But because from his intense desire he still importuned to be let into heaven, he was sent into a society of upright spirits of this earth; but they also said that he could not be with them. He was of a black color in the light of heaven, but he said that he was not of a black, but of a brown color. It was told me that they are such at first, who are afterward received among those that constitute the province of the seminal vesicles in the Greatest Man, or heaven; for in those vesicles the semen is collected and enclosed around with a suitable material, fitted for preserving the prolific principle of the semen from being dissipated, but such as may be thrown off in the neck of the uterus, that thus what is reserved within may serve for conception, or for the impregnation of the ovulum. Hence also that seminal matter has an effort, and as it were a burning desire, to throw itself off and leave the semen to perform its use, similar to what was seen with that spirit. He still came to me, in vile garments, and said again that he burned to come into heaven, and that he now perceived that he was such that he could. I was then permitted to tell him, that perhaps this was an indication that he would shortly be received. He was then told by angels to cast off his garment, which from his desire he rejected so quickly, that scarce anything could be quicker. By this was represented what are the desires of those who are in the province to which the seminal vesicles correspond. It was said that these spirits when prepared for heaven, put off their garments and are clothed with shining new ones, and become angels. They were likened to caterpillars, which having passed through their vile state, are changed into chrysalises, and thus into butterflies; to which another dress is then given, and also wings of a blue, yellow, silver, or golden color; and then the liberty of flying in the air as in their heaven, of celebrating their marriages and laying their eggs, and thus of providing for the propagation of their kind; and at the same time there is allotted them sweet and pleasant food from the juices and odors of the various flowers.

80 Thus far nothing has been said of the quality of the angels who are from that earth; for those who come to the men of their earth and sit at their head, as mentioned above (n. 73), are not angels in their interior heaven, but are angelic spirits, or angels, in their exterior heaven. And as the nature of the angels of the interior heaven has also been disclosed to me, it is permitted to relate what has been given me to know. A certain one of the spirits of Jupiter who inspire fear, applied himself to my left side under the elbow and spoke thence. But his speech was harsh, nor were his words sufficiently distinct and separate; so that I had to wait some time before I could gather his meaning. And when he spoke he also injected something of fear, thus also admonishing me to receive the angels well when they came. But it was given to answer, that this did not depend on me; since all were received with me as they are. Presently angels of that earth came to me, and I was able to perceive from their speech with me, that they were altogether different from the angels of our earth; for their speech was not by words, but by ideas, which diffused themselves everywhere through my interiors, and thus they had also an influx into my face, so that the face concurred in every particular, beginning from the lips and proceeding in every direction toward the circumference. The ideas which were in the place of spoken words were discrete, though in small degree. They afterwards spoke with me by ideas still less discrete, so that scarce any interstice was perceivable. To my perception it was like the meaning of words with those who only attend to the meaning abstractly from the words. This speech was more intelligible to me than the former, and was also more full. Like the former it flowed into the face, but the influx in accordance with the quality of the speech, was more continuous. It did not however begin like the former from the lips, but from the eyes. Afterward they spoke still more continuously and fully, so that my face was not then able to concur by fitting motion; but there was felt an influx into the brain, and that this was then acted upon in like manner. At last they so spoke that the discourse fell only into the interior understanding. Its volubility was like that of a thin aura. I felt the influx itself, but not distinctly the particulars. These kinds of speech were like fluids, the first kind like flowing water, the second like thinner water, the third comparatively like the atmosphere, and the fourth like a thin aura. The spirit mentioned above, who was on the left side, sometimes interrupted, especially warning me to act modestly with his angels; for there were spirits from our earth, who introduced such things as were displeasing. He said that he did not at first understand what the angels said, but that he did afterward when he was brought nearer to my left ear. Then also his speech was not harsh, as before, but like that of other spirits.

81 I afterward spoke with these angels about some notable things on our earth, especially about the art of printing, about the Word, and about the various doctrines of the church from the Word; and I said that the Word and the doctrines are published, and so are learned. They wondered exceedingly that such things could be published by writing and by types.

82 I was permitted to see how the spirits of that earth after they have been prepared, are taken up into heaven and become angels. There then appear chariots and horses bright as with fire, by which they are carried away like Elijah. Chariots and horses bright as with fire appear, because it is thus represented that they have been instructed and prepared to enter heaven; since "chariots" signify the doctrinals of the church, and "bright horses" the understanding enlightened.[9]

83 The heaven into which they are taken, appears on the right of their earth, thus apart from the heaven of the angels of our earth. The angels who are in that heaven appear clothed in shining blue, dotted with small golden stars, and this because they loved that color in the world. They also believed that it was the veriest celestial color, chiefly because they are in such good of love as that color corresponds to.[10]

---

[9] "Chariots" signify the doctrinals of the church (n. 2761, 5321, 8215). "Horses" signify the intellectual faculty (n. 2760, 2761, 2762, 3217, 5321, 6125, 6400, 6534, 7024, 8146, 8148, 8351). "The white horse" in the *Apocalypse* signifies the understanding of the word (n. 2760). By "Elijah" in the representative sense is meant the word (n. 2762, 5247). And because all the doctrine of the church and the understanding of it are from the word, Elijah was called "the chariot of Israel and the horsemen thereof" (n. 2762). He was therefore taken up by a fiery chariot and horses of fire (n. 2762, 8029).

[10] Blue from red or flame corresponds to the good of celestial love, and blue from white or light corresponds to the good of spiritual love (n. 9868).

84 There appeared to me a bald head, but only the top of it, which was bony; and it was said that those who are to die within a year see such a one, and that they then prepare themselves. They do not fear death there, except on account of leaving the consort, children or parents; for they know that they will live after death, and that they are not going out of life, because they are going into heaven. Therefore they do not call it dying, but being heaven-made. Those who have lived in love truly conjugial on that earth, and have taken care of their children as becomes parents, do not die of diseases, but tranquilly as in sleep; and thus they migrate from the world into heaven. The age of men there is usually thirty years, according to the years of our earth. The cause of their dying in so short a time is of the Lord's providence, lest the multitude of men should increase beyond what can be sustained by that earth; and because after they have fulfilled those years, they do not suffer themselves to be led by spirits and angels as those do who have not yet fulfilled them; for which reason spirits and angels rarely go to the more mature. They come to maturity also more quickly than on our earth. Even in the first flower of youth they form marriages, and then their delights are to love the consort, and to take care of their children. Other delights they indeed call delights, but respectively external.

FOUR

The Planet Mars

85 THE SPIRITS OF MARS ARE THE BEST OF ALL AMONG the spirits who are from the earths of our solar system, for they are as to the most part celestial men, not unlike those who were of the Most Ancient Church on this earth.[1] When they are represented as to their quality, they are represented with the face in heaven and the body in the world of spirits; and those of them who are angels, with the face toward the Lord and the body in heaven.

86 The planet Mars in the idea of spirits and angels, like the other planets, appears constantly in its place, which is to the left in front, at some distance, in the plane of the breast, and so out of the sphere where the spirits of our earth are. The spirits of one earth are separate from the spirits of another earth, because the spirits of each earth refer to some particular province in the Greatest Man, and hence are in another and different state; and diversity of state makes them appear separate from each other, either to the right or to the left, at a greater or less distance.[2]

---

[1] The First and Most Ancient Church on this earth which was celestial church, which is the primary of all, see (n. 607, 895, 920, 1121-1124, 2896, 4493, 8891, 9942, 10,545). The church is called celestial in which the principal thing is love to the Lord, but spiritual in which the principal thing is charity toward the neighbor and faith (n. 3691, 6435, 9468, 9680, 9683, 9780).

[2] Distances in the other life are real appearances, which are presented by the Lord to be seen, according to the state of the interiors of angels and spirits (n. 5604, 9104, 9440, 10,146).

87 Spirits from Mars came to me and applied themselves to my left temple, where they breathed upon me with their speech; but I did not understand it. It was soft in its flow, softer I had never before perceived; it was like the softest aura. It first breathed upon my left temple, and upon my left ear from above; and the breathing proceeded thence to my left eye, and little by little to the right, and then flowed down, chiefly from the left eye to the lips; and when it reached the lips, it entered through the mouth, and through the passage within the mouth, and indeed through the Eustachian tube, into the brain. When the breathing arrived there, I then understood their speech; and it was granted to speak with them. I observed when they were speaking with me, that my lips were moved, and the tongue also a little; which was by reason of the correspondence of interior speech with exterior speech. Exterior speech is that of articulate sound finding its way to the external membrane of the ear, whence it is conveyed, by means of little organs, membranes, and fibers which are within the ear, into the brain. From this, it was granted, to know that the speech of the inhabitants of Mars was different from that of the inhabitants of our earth, namely, it was not sonorous, but almost tacit, insinuating itself into the interior hearing and sight by a shorter way; and being such it was more perfect, and more full of the ideas of thought, thus approaching nearer to the speech of spirits and angels. The very affection of the speech is also represented with them in the face, and its thought in the eyes; for the thought and the speech, also the affection and the face, with them act as one. They regard it as nefarious to think one thing and speak another, and to will one thing and show another in the face. They do not know what hypocrisy is, nor what fraudulent pretence and deceit are. That such was also the speech of the most ancient people on our earth, it has been given me to know by conversation with some of them in the other life; and that this matter may be made clearer, it is permitted to relate what I have heard, as follows: "It was shown me by an influx which I cannot describe, what kind of speech they had who were of the Most Ancient Church, namely, that it was not articulate, like the vocal speech of our time, but tacit, which was effected not by external respiration but by internal; thus it was the speech of thought. It was also granted to perceive what their internal respiration was, that it proceeded from the navel toward the heart, and so through the lips without being sonorous when they spoke; and that it did not enter into the ear of another by the external way, and beat upon what is called the drum of the ear, but by a certain internal way, and in fact by a certain passage now called the Eustachian tube. It was shown that by such speech they could much more fully express the feelings of the mind and the ideas of the thought, than can ever be done by articulate sounds or sonorous words; which speech is in like manner directed by respiration, but external: for there is no word, nor indeed anything in a word, which is not directed by applications of the respiration. But with them this was much more perfect, because it was effected by internal respiration, which is the more perfect, because more internal, and more applicable and better conformed to the very ideas of thought; and it is further effected also by the little motions of the lips and corresponding changes of the face. For, since they were celestial men, whatever they thought shone forth from their face and eyes, which were varied in conformity, the face as to form according to the life of the affection, and the eyes as to light. They could by no means present any other countenance than such as accorded with what they thought; and because they had speech by internal respiration, which is that of man's spirit itself, they were therefore able to associate and speak with angels. The respiration of the spirits of Mars was also communicated to me;[3] and it was perceived that it proceeded from the region of the thorax toward the navel, and thence flowed upward through the chest with an imperceptible breathing toward the mouth. From this, as also from other proofs of experience, it was made plain to me that they were of a celestial genius; thus that they were not unlike those who were from the Most Ancient Church on this earth.

88 I have been instructed that the spirits of Mars have reference in the Greatest Man to what is mediate between the intellectual and the voluntary faculties, thus to *thought from affection*; and the best of them to *the affection of thought*. It is for this reason that their face acts as one with their thought, and that they cannot dissemble before any one. And as they have reference to this in the Greatest Man, the

---

[3] That spirits and angels have respiration (n. 3884, 3885, 3891, 3893).

middle province, which is between the cerebrum and the cerebellum, corresponds to them. For with those with whom the cerebrum and the cerebellum are conjoined as to spiritual operations, the face acts as one with the thought; so that the very affection of the thought shines forth from the face, and from the affection, with the aid of some signs going forth from the eyes, the general of thought shines forth. For this reason when the spirits of Mars were with me, I perceived sensibly a drawing back of the front part of the head toward the occiput, thus of the cerebrum toward the cerebellum.[4]

89 Once when the spirits of Mars were with me, and occupied the sphere of my mind, some spirits from our earth came and wished to infuse themselves also into that sphere. But then these spirits from our earth became as it were insane, for the reason that they did not at all agree. For the spirits of our earth in the Greatest Man have reference to the external sense, and thus they were in an idea turned to the world and to self, while the spirits of Mars were in an idea turned from self to heaven and to the neighbor; hence there was contrariety. But angelic spirits of Mars then came, and at their approach communication was taken away, and so the spirits of our earth withdrew.

90 The angelic spirits spoke with me about the life of the inhabitants on their earth, that they are not under empires, but are arranged in societies larger and smaller, and that they consociate with themselves in their societies such as agree with them in mind, which they know at once from the face and speech, and are rarely deceived. Then they are friends at once. They said also that their consociations are delightful, and that they speak with one another of those things that are done in the societies, especially those done in heaven; for many of them have manifest communication with the angels of heaven. Those in their societies who begin to think perversely, and from this to will evil, are dissociated, and left to themselves alone, and thus they pass their time very miserably out of the society, among rocks or elsewhere; for the society no longer has a care over them. Certain

---

[4] Human faces on our earth in ancient times received influx from the cerebellum, and the faces then acted as one with the interior affections of man but that afterward they received influx from the cerebrum, when man began to dissemble and counterfeit in the face affections not his own, and concerning the changes brought upon faces therefrom in process of time (n. 4325-4328).

societies try in various ways to compel such to repentance; but when they cannot effect this, they separate themselves from them. Thus they take care lest the lust of dominion and the lust of gain creep in; that is, lest any from the lust of dominion subject any society to themselves, and then many more; and lest any from the lust of gain seize the goods of others. Every one there lives content with his own goods, and every one with his own honor, in being esteemed just and one that loves his neighbor. This delight and tranquillity of mind would perish, if those that think and will what is evil were not cast out, and if the love of self and the love of the world were not met prudently and severely in the very beginnings. For these are the loves for the sake of which empires and kingdoms have been established, within which there are few who do not wish to have dominion, and to possess the goods of others. For there are few who do what is just and equitable from the love of what is just and equitable; still less who do what is good from charity itself, rather than from fear of the law, of life, of the loss of gain, of honor, and of reputation on account of those things.

91 Concerning the Divine worship of those that dwell on their earth, they said that they acknowledge and adore our Lord, saying that He is the Only God, and that He rules both heaven and the universe; and that all good is from Him, and that He leads them; also that He often appears with them on their earth. It was then granted to say to them, that Christians also on our earth know that the Lord rules heaven and earth, from the words of the Lord Himself in *Matthew:*

> All power is given unto Me in heaven and in earth (28:18)

but that they do not believe this as those who are from the earth Mars do. They said also that there they believe that there is nothing in them but what is filthy and infernal, and that all good is the Lord's, yea, saying further, that of themselves they are devils, and that the Lord draws them out of hell, and continually withholds them. Once when the Lord was named, I saw that those spirits humbled themselves so interiorly and profoundly as cannot be described; for in their humiliation they had the thought that they were of themselves in hell; and that so they were altogether unworthy to look to the Lord, Who is holiness Itself. They were so profoundly in that thought, from belief, that they were as if out of themselves; and they remained in it upon their knees until the Lord lifted them up, and then as it were drew them out of hell. When they thus come forth out of their humiliation, they are full of good and of love, and thence of joy of heart. When they so humble themselves, they do not turn their face to the Lord, for this they do not then dare to do, but turn it away. The spirits who were around me said that they had never seen such humiliation.

92 Certain spirits who were from that earth wondered that there were about me so many spirits from hell, and that they also spoke with me. But it was given to answer, that this was permitted them in order that I might know their quality, and why they are in hell, and that this is according to their life. It was also given to say that there were many among them whom I had known when they lived in the world, and that some were then established in great dignity, who yet had nothing but the world in their heart; but that no evil spirit, even the most infernal, could do me any harm, because I was continually protected by the Lord.

93 There was presented before me an inhabitant of that earth. He was not indeed an inhabitant, but like one. His face was like that of the inhabitants of our earth, but the lower region of the face was black, not from a beard, for he had none, but from blackness in place of it. This blackness extended on both sides as far as the ears. The upper part of the face was yellowish, like the faces of the inhabitants of our earth who are not altogether white. These spirits said further that in their earth they feed on the fruits of trees, especially a certain round fruit which grows up out of the ground, and also leguminous plants. That they are there clothed with garments made out of fibers of the bark of certain trees. These have such consistence that they can be woven, and also glued together by a kind of gum which they have with them. They further related that they know there how to make fluid fires from which they have light during the evening and night.

94 I saw a most beautiful flame of varying color, purple, and also bright red, and the colors with a beautiful ruddy glow from the flame, I also saw a certain hand, to which this flame adhered, at first on the back, afterward in the palm, and thence it played round the hand on all sides. This lasted for some little time. Then the hand with its flamy light was removed to a distance, and where it rested there was a bright light. In that brightness the hand receded, and then the flame was changed into a bird, which at first was of the same colors as the flame, and the colors glittering in like manner; but gradually the colors were changed, and with the colors the vigor of life in the bird. It flew round about and at first around my head, then forward into a certain narrow chamber, which appeared like a shrine; and as it flew farther forward, so its life receded, till at length it became as of stone, at first of a pearl color, afterward dark; but though without life, it was still flying. When the bird was flying around my head and was still in the vigor of life, a spirit was seen rising from below through the region of the loins to the region of the breast, who wished to take the bird away. But because it was so beautiful, the spirits around me prevented him; for their eyes were all fastened on it. The spirit however who rose up from below, endeavored strongly to persuade them that the Lord was with him, and thus that he did this from the Lord. And then, though most of them did not believe this, they no longer prevented him from taking away the bird. But as heaven flowed in at that moment, he could not hold it, and presently let it go free out of his hand. When this was done, the spirits around me who had intently watched the bird and its successive changes, spoke with one another about it, and this for a considerable time. They perceived that such a sight could not but signify something celestial. They knew that the flame signified celestial love and its affections; that the hand to which the flame adhered, signified life and its power; the changes of colors, varieties of life as to wisdom and intelligence; and the bird also the same, but with the difference that the flame signified celestial love and the things of that love, and the bird signified spiritual love and the things of that love (celestial love is love to the Lord, and spiritual love charity toward the neighbor), and that the changes of the colors and at the same time of the life in the bird, until it became as of stone, signified successive changes of spiritual life as to intelligence. They knew also that spirits who ascend from below through the region of the loins to the region of the breast, are in a strong persuasion that they are in the Lord, and hence believe that all things they do, even though evil, they do by the Lord's will. But yet they could not know from this who were meant by this appearance. At length they were instructed from heaven that the inhabitants of Mars were meant, that their celestial love, in which very many still are, was signified by the flame which adhered to the hand, and that the bird in the beginning, when in the beauty of its colors and the vigor of its life, signified their spiritual love; but that the bird's becoming as of stone without life, and at length of a dark color, signified such of the inhabitants as have removed themselves from the good of love and are in evil, and yet still believe that they are in the Lord. The same was signified by the spirit who rose up and wished to take away the bird.

95 By the bird of stone were also represented the inhabitants of that earth who in a strange manner transmute the life of their thoughts and affections into almost no life, concerning which I have heard as follows. There was a certain spirit above my head who spoke with me, and from the sound of his voice it was perceived that he was as it were in a state of sleep. In this state he spoke many things, and with such prudence that if he were awake he could not speak more prudently. It was given to perceive that he was a subject through which angels spoke; and that in that state he perceived and brought forth what they said,[5] for he spoke nothing but what was true. If anything flowed in from any other source, he admitted it indeed, but did not bring it forth. I questioned him about his state, and he said that this state was to him peaceful, and without any anxiety about the future; and that at the same time he performed uses, whereby he had communication with heaven. It was told me that such spirits in the Greatest Man have reference to the longitudinal sinus in the brain, which lies between its two hemispheres, and there he is in a quiet state, however the brain may be disturbed on both sides. When I was in conversation with this spirit, some spirits introduced themselves toward the fore part of the head, where he was, and pressed

---

[5] That communications are made through spirits sent forth by societies of spirits and angels to other societies, and that these emissary spirits are called subjects (n. 4403, 5856, 5983, 5985-5989).

upon him; wherefore he withdrew to one side, and gave them place. The newly arrived spirits conversed with one another; but neither the spirits around me, nor I myself, understood what they were saying. I was instructed by angels that they were spirits from the earth Mars, who were skilled in talking with one another in such manner that the spirits present neither understood nor perceived anything. I wondered that such speech was possible, because all spirits have one kind of speech, which flows from the thought, and consists of ideas, that are heard as words in the spiritual world. It was said that those spirits form in a certain manner ideas expressed by the lips and the face, not intelligible to others, and at the same moment artfully withdraw their thoughts, taking special care that nothing of the affection should manifest itself, because if anything of the affection were perceived, the thought would then be manifest; for the thought flows from the affection, and is as it were in it. I was instructed further that the inhabitants of the earth Mars who place heavenly life in knowledges alone, and not in a life of love, contrived such speech, though not all of them; and that when they become spirits, they retain it. It is these who were signified in particular by the bird of stone; for to present speech by modifications of the countenance and foldings of the lips, with the removal of the affections and withdrawal of the thoughts from others, is to take the soul out of speech, and to render it like a mere image, and by degrees they also become similar. But although they think that they are not understood by others in what they say among themselves, still angelic spirits perceive each and everything that they speak, for the reason that from them no thought can be concealed. This was also shown them by living experience. I was thinking of this, that the evil spirits of our earth are not affected with shame when they infest others, and this thought flowed in with me from angelic spirits who perceived their speech. These spirits of Mars then acknowledged that this was what they were speaking of among themselves, and they marveled. Moreover, there were many things disclosed by an angelic spirit, both of what they spoke and of what they were thinking, notwithstanding they endeavored to withdraw their thoughts from him. Afterward those spirits flowed in from above into my face, and their influx was felt like a fine striated rain, which was a sign that they were not in any affection of truth and good, since that is represented by what is striated. They then spoke with me plainly, saying that the inhabitants of their earth speak with one another in like manner. It was then said to them, that this is evil, because in this way they obstruct internals, and recede from them to externals, which they also deprive of their life; and especially because it is not sincere to speak thus. For they who are sincere have no wish to speak nor even to think anything but what others may know, yea all, even the whole heaven. But they who do not wish others to know what they speak, judge concerning others, think evil of them, and well of themselves, and are at length carried by habit so far as to think and speak ill of the church, of heaven, and even of the Lord Himself. It was said that they who love knowledges, and not so much a life according to them, have reference to the interior membrane of the skull in the Greatest Man; but they who accustom themselves to speak without affection, and to draw the thought to themselves and withdraw it from others, have reference to that membrane when it is become bony, because from having some spiritual life they come to have no life.

96 As those who are in knowledges alone, and in no life of love, were also represented by the bird of stone, and as they have thence no spiritual life, I may therefore show here, by way of appendix, that those alone have spiritual life who are in heavenly love, and in knowledges therefrom; and that a love contains in itself all the power of knowing which is of that love. For example, the animals of the earth, and also the animals of the air, or the birds, have the knowledge of all things that are of their loves. These loves are, to nourish themselves, to dwell in safety, to propagate offspring, to bring up their young, and with some, to provide for themselves against winter. Consequently they have all the requisite knowledge, for this is in those loves, and it flows into them as into its very receptacles; which knowledge with some animals is such, that man cannot but be astonished. The knowledge is innate with them, and is called instinct; but it is of the natural love in which they are. If man were in his love, which is love to God and toward the neighbor (for this love is man's proper love, by which he is distinguished from the beasts, and is heavenly love), man would then be not only in all requisite knowledge, but also in all intelligence and wisdom; for these would flow into those loves from heaven, that is, through heaven from the Divine. But because man is not born into those loves, but into the opposite ones, namely, into the loves of self and the world, for that reason he cannot but be born into all ignorance and lack of knowledge. But by Divine means he is led on to something of intelligence and wisdom, yet not actually into anything of it, unless the love, of self and the world are removed, and the way is thus opened for love to God and the neighbor. That love to God and love toward the neighbor have in them all intelligence and wisdom, may be evident from those who in the world have been in these loves. When after death they come into heaven, they there come into such knowledge and wisdom as they had never known before; yea, they think and speak there, as do the rest of the angels, such things as the ear has never heard, nor the mind has ever known, and which are ineffable. The reason is, that those loves have in them the faculty of receiving such things.

FIVE

The Planet Saturn

97 THE SPIRITS FROM THE EARTH SATURN APPEAR IN FRONT at a considerable distance, beneath in the plane of the knees, where the earth itself is; and when the eye is opened to see thither, a multitude of spirits come into view who are all from that earth. They are seen on this part of that earth, and to the right of it. It has also been granted to speak with them, and thereby to know their quality in comparison with others. They are upright and modest, and inasmuch as they esteem themselves little, therefore they also appear small in the other life.

98 In worship they are exceedingly humble, for in it they account themselves as nothing. They worship our Lord, and acknowledge Him as the only God. The Lord also appears to them at times under an angelic form, and thereby as a Man, and the Divine then shines forth from the face and affects the mind. The inhabitants also, when they arrive at a certain age, speak with spirits, by whom they are instructed concerning the Lord, how He ought to be worshiped, and likewise how they ought to live. When any wish to seduce the spirits who come from the earth Saturn, and to withdraw them from faith in the Lord, or from humiliation towards Him, and from uprightness of life, they say they wish to die. There then appear in their hands small knives, with which they seem desirous of striking their breasts, On being questioned why they do so, they say that they would rather die than be drawn away from the Lord. The spirits of our earth sometimes deride them on this account, and infest them with reproaches for so doing. But they reply, that they know well that they do not kill themselves, and that this is only an appearance flowing from the will of their mind, inclining them rather to die than to be withdrawn from the worship of the Lord.

99 They said that sometimes spirits from our earth come to them, and ask them what God they worship; to whom they reply, that they are insane, and that there cannot be a greater proof of insanity than to ask what God any one worships, when there is but one only God for all in the universe; and that they are still more insane in this, that they do not acknowledge the Lord to be that one only God, and that He rules the entire heaven, and thereby the whole world; for whosoever rules heaven also rules the world, inasmuch as the world is ruled through heaven.

100 They said that on their earth there are also some who call the nocturnal light, which is great, the Lord; but that they are separated from the rest, and are not tolerated by them. That nocturnal light comes from the great bolt, which at a distance encompasses that earth, and from the moons which are called Saturn's satellites.

101 They related further that another kind of spirits, who go in companies, frequently come to them, desiring to know how things are with them; and that by various methods they draw out from them whatever they know. They said concerning these spirits, that they were not insane, only in this, that they desire to know so much for no other use than to know. They were afterwards instructed that these spirits were from the planet Mercury, or the earth nearest the sun, and that they are delighted with knowledges alone, and not so much with their uses.

102 The inhabitants and spirits of the planet Saturn have relation in the Greatest Man, to the *middle sense between the spiritual and the natural man,* but to that which recedes from the natural and accedes to the spiritual. Hence it is that those spirits appear to be carried or snatched away into heaven, and presently to be let back again; for whatever appertains to the spiritual sense is in heaven; but whatever appertains to the natural sense is beneath heaven. Inasmuch as the spirits of our earth, in the Greatest Man have relation to natural and corporeal sense, it was given me to know by manifest experience how the spiritual man and the natural fight and strive with each other, when the latter is not in faith and charity. The spirits of the earth Saturn came from afar into view, and there was then opened a living communication between them and such spirits of our earth. The latter, on thus perceiving the former, became as if insane, and began to infest them, by infusing unworthy suggestions concerning faith, and also concerning the Lord; and whilst abusing them with these invectives and insults, they also cast themselves into the midst of them, and from the insanity in which they were, they endeavored to do evil to them. But the spirits of Saturn feared nothing, because they were secure and in tranquillity; whereas the spirits of our earth, when they were in the midst of them, began to be tortured, and to respire with difficulty, and so they cast themselves out, one in this way and another that, till they all disappeared. The spirits who were present perceived from this, what is the quality of the natural man when separate from the spiritual, and when he comes into a spiritual sphere, namely, that he is insane; for the natural man separate from the spiritual is wise only from the world, and not from heaven; and he who is wise only from the world, believes nothing but what be can apprehend with his senses, and the things which he believes he believes from the fallacies of the senses, which, unless they are removed by an influx from the spiritual world, produce falsities. Hence it is that spiritual things to him are not anything, insomuch that he can scarcely bear to hear mention made of anything spiritual; wherefore such become insane when they are kept in a spiritual sphere. It is otherwise during their abode in the world, where they either think naturally concerning spiritual things, or avert their ears that they may not hear them; that is, they hear and do not attend. It was also manifest from this experience, that the natural man cannot introduce himself into the spiritual, that is, ascend; but when man is in faith, and thereby in spiritual life, in this case the spiritual man flows into the natural, and thinks therein. For there is given a spiritual influx, that is, an influx from the spiritual world into the natural, but not the reverse.[1]

103 I was further informed by the spirits of that earth respecting the inhabitants, what their consociations are, with several other particulars. They said that they live distinguished into families, every family apart by itself; each family consisting of a man and his wife with their children; and the children, when they enter the married state, are separated from the parental house, and have no further care about it. Wherefore the spirits from that earth appear two and two. They are little solicitous about food and raiment, they feed on the fruits and legumes their earth produces; and they are clothed slightly, being encompassed with a coarse skin or coat, which repels the cold. Moreover, all on that earth know that they will live after death; and that on this account also they make light of their bodies, only so far as regards that life, which they say is to remain and serve the Lord. It is for this reason likewise that they do not bury the bodies of the dead, but cast them forth, and cover them with branches of forest trees.

104 They were asked concerning that great belt, which appears from our earth to rise above the horizon of that planet, and to vary its situations. They said, that it does not appear to them as a belt, but only as a snowy light in the heaven in various directions.

---

[1] Influx is spiritual, and not physical or natural, consequently influx is from the spiritual world into the natural, and not from the natural into the spiritual (n. 3219, 5119, 5259, 5427, 5428, 5477, 6322). It appears as if influx is from externals into man's internals, but this is a fallacy (n. 3721).

SIX

The Planet Venus

105 THE EARTH OR PLANET VENUS, ITS SPIRITS AND INHABITANTS. The planet Venus, in the idea of spirits and angels, appears to the left a little backwards, at some distance from our earth. It is said, in the idea of spirits, because neither the sun of this world, nor any planet, appears to any spirit; but spirits have only an idea that they exist. It is in consequence of such idea that the sun of this world is presented behind as something quite dark, and the planets not movable as in the world, but remaining constantly in their several places; see above (n.42).

106 In the planet Venus there are two kinds of men, of dispositions opposite to each other; the first mild and humane, the second savage and almost like wild beasts. They who are mild and humane appear on the further side of the earth, they who are savage and like wild beasts, appear on the side looking this way. But it is to be known that they appear thus according to the states of their life, for in the spiritual world the state of life determines every appearance of space and of distance.

107 Some of those who appear on the further side of the planet, and who are mild and humane, came to me and were presented visibly above the head, and I spoke with them on various subjects. Amongst other things, they said that during their abode in the world, and more so since they were become spirits, they acknowledged our Lord as their only God. They added that on their earth they had seen Him, and they represented also how they had seen Him. These spirits in the Greatest Man have relation to *the memory of things material, agreeing with the memory of things immaterial,* to which the spirits of Mercury have relation: wherefore the spirits of Mercury have the fullest agreement with these spirits of Venus, and on this account, when they were together, a remarkable change, and a powerful operation in my brain, was perceivable from their influx; see above (n. 43).

108 But I did not speak with those spirits who are on the side that looks this way, and who are savage and almost like wild beasts; but I was informed by the angels concerning their quality, and whence they have so fierce a nature. The cause is this, that they are exceedingly delighted with rapine, and more especially with eating their plunder; the delight thence arising, when they think about eating their plunder, was communicated to me, and was perceived to be most extraordinary. That on our earth there have been inhabitants of a like fierce nature, appears from the histories of various nations; also from the inhabitants of the land of Canaan (1 *Sam.* 30.16); and likewise from the Jewish and Israelitish nation, even in the time of David, in that they made yearly excursions, and plundered the Gentiles, and rejoiced in feasting on the spoils. I was informed further, that those inhabitants are for the most part giants, and that the men of our earth reach only to their navels; also that they are stupid, making no inquiries concerning heaven or eternal life, but immersed solely in earthly cares and the care of their cattle.

109 Because they are such, when they come into the other life they are exceedingly infested there by evils and falsities. The hells, which appertain to them, appear near their earth, and have no communication with the hells of the wicked of our earth, because they differ altogether in genius and disposition: hence also their evils and falsities are altogether of a different sort.

110 Such, however, amongst them, as can be saved, are in places of vastation, and are there reduced to the last state of desperation; for there is no other method whereby evils and false persuasions of that kind can be subdued and removed. When they are in a state of desperation, they cry out that they are beasts, that they are abominations; that they are hatreds, and that thus they are damned. Some of them, when they are in this state, exclaim even against heaven; but as this proceeds from desperation, it is forgiven them. The Lord moderates that in their vituperations they may not pour them forth except to certain limits. These, when they have passed through extreme suffering, are finally saved, inasmuch as corporeal things with them are as if dead. It was further declared concerning these spirits, that during their life on their earth they believed in a certain Supreme Creator without a Mediator; but when they are saved, they are also instructed that the Lord alone is God, the Savior and Mediator. I have seen some of them, after they have passed through extreme suffering, taken up into heaven; and when they were received there, I have perceived such a tenderness of joy from them as drew tears from my eyes.

SEVEN

The Moon

111 CERTAIN SPIRITS APPEARED ABOVE THE HEAD, AND thence were heard voices like thunder; for they thundered with their voices like the thunder from the clouds after lightning. I asserted that it was a great multitude of spirits, who had the art of uttering voices attended with so loud a noise. The more simple spirits who were with me laughed at them, at which I greatly wondered. The cause of their laughter was presently discovered to be this, that the spirits who thundered were not many, but few, and were also as small as boys; and that before they had terrified them by such noises, and yet were unable to do them any harm. In order that I might know their quality, some of them let themselves down from on high where they were thundering; and what surprised me, one carried another on his back, and thus two of them approached me. Their faces appeared not unhandsome, but longer than the faces of other spirits. Their stature was like the stature of boys seven years old, but more robust; thus they were dwarfs. It was told me by the angels, that they were from the Moon. He who was carried on the other's back, on coming to me, applied himself to my left side under the elbow, and thence spoke with me, saying that whenever they utter their voices they thus thunder; and that thereby they terrify the spirits who wish to do them evil; and put some to flight, and that thus they go with security whithersoever they will. That I might know certainly that they made this sound, he retired from me to some others, but not entirely out of sight, and thundered in like manner. They showed, moreover, that the voice being uttered from the abdomen, like an eructation, made this thundering sound. It was perceived that this was owing to the fact, that the inhabitants of the Moon do not speak from the lungs like the inhabitants of other earths, but from the abdomen, and thus from some air there collected, by reason that the Moon is not encompassed with an atmosphere like that of other earths. I was instructed that the spirits of the Moon, in the Greatest Man, have relation to the ensiform or zyphoid cartilage, to which the ribs in front are joined, and from which descends the *facia alba,* which is the fulcrum of the abdominal muscles.

112 That there are also inhabitants on the Moon, spirits and angels know, and in like manner that there are inhabitants on the moons or satellites which revolve about the earths Jupiter and Saturn. They who have not seen and spoken with spirits therefrom, still do not doubt but that there are also men upon them, because they are equally earths; and where there is an earth, there are men; for man is the end for which every earth was created, and nothing was made by the Great Creator without an end. That the human race is the end of creation, that from it there may be a heaven, may appear to every one who thinks from a somewhat enlightened reason.

EIGHT

Reasons Why the Lord was Born on Our Earth

113 THERE ARE MANY REASONS, CONCERNING WHICH I HAD information from heaven, why it pleased the Lord to be born and to assume the human on our earth, and not on another. The PRINCIPLE REASON *was because of the Word, in that it might be written on our earth; and when written be afterwards published throughout the whole earth; and when once published be preserved to all posterity; and that thus it might be made manifest, even to all in the other life, that God became Man.*

114 *That the principal reason was because of the Word,* is because the Word is the Divine truth itself, which teaches man that there is a God, that there is a heaven and a hell, and that there is a life after death; and teaches moreover how man ought to live and believe, in order to come into heaven, and thus into eternal happiness. All these things would have been altogether unknown without a revelation, thus on this earth without the Word; and yet man is so created that, as to his interiors, he cannot die.[1]

---

[1] From natural light alone nothing is known concerning the Lord, concerning heaven and hell, concerning the life of man after death, and concerning Divine truths, by which man has

115 *That the Word might be written on our earth,* is because the art of writing has existed here from the most ancient time, first on the bark of trees, next on parchment, afterwards on paper, and lastly published by types. This was provided by the Lord for the sake of the Word.

116 *That the Word might afterwards be published through out the whole earth,* is because there is commerce here between all nations, both by land and water, to all parts of the globe; hence that the Word once written might be conveyed from one nation to another, and be taught everywhere.

117 *That the Word once written might be preserved to all posterity,* consequently for thousands and thousands of years, and that it has been so preserved is well known.

118 *That thus it might be made manifest that God became Man;* for this is the first and most essential, for the sake of which the Word was revealed. For no one can believe in God, and love God, whom he cannot comprehend under some appearance; wherefore they who acknowledge what is invisible and thus incomprehensible, in thought sink into nature, and thus believe in no God. Hence it pleased the Lord to be born on this earth, and to make this manifest by the Word, that it might not only be known on this globe, but also might be made manifest thereby to spirits and angels even from other earths, and likewise to the Gentiles from our own earth.[2]

119 It is to be known that the Word on our earth, given through heaven from the Lord, is the union of heaven and the world; for which end there is a correspondence of all things contained in the letter of the Word with the Divine things in heaven; and the Word in its supreme and inmost sense treats of the Lord, of His kingdom in the heavens and the earths, and of love and faith from Him and

---

spiritual and eternal life (n. 8944, 10,318-10,320). This may appear from this, that many, and among them the learned, do not believe those things, although they are born where the word is, and where there is instruction by the Word concerning those things (n. 10,319). Therefore it was necessary there should be a revelation from heaven, because man was born for heaven (n. 1775).

  [2] The Gentiles in the other life are instructed by angels, and they who have lived well according to their religious principles, receive the truths of faith, and acknowledge the Lord (n. 2049, 2595, 2598, 2600, 2601, 2603, 2661, 2863, 3263).

in Him, consequently of life from Him and in Him. Such things are presented to the angels in heaven, when the Word of our earth is read and preached.[3]

120 In every other earth Divine truth is manifested by word of mouth through spirits and angels, as was said above in speaking of the inhabitants of the earths of this solar system. But this manifestation is confined within families; for the human race in most earths live distinct according to families; wherefore the Divine truth thus revealed through spirits and angels is not conveyed far beyond the limits of families, and unless a new revelation constantly succeeds, truth is either perverted or perishes. It is otherwise on our earth, where the Divine truth, which is the Word, remains for ever in its integrity.

121 It is to be known that the Lord acknowledges and receives all, of whatsoever earth they be, who acknowledge and worship God under the human form, inasmuch as God under the human form is the Lord. And because the Lord appears to the inhabitants in the earths in an angelic form, which is the human form, therefore when the spirits and angels from those earths are informed by the spirits and angels of our earth that God is actually Man, they receive that Word, acknowledge it, and rejoice that it is so.

122 To the reasons above adduced, may be added, that the inhabitants and spirits of our earth, in the Greatest Man, have relation to the natural and external sense, which sense is the ultimate wherein the interiors of life close, and rest as on their common basis. The case is similar in regard to the Divine truth in the letter, which is called the Word, and which for this reason also was given on this earth, and not on any other:[4] and because the Lord is the Word, and

---

[3] The word is understood by the angels in the heavens differently from what it is understood by men on the earths, and that the internal or spiritual sense is for the angels but the external or natural sense for men (n. 1769-1772, 1887, 2143, 2333, 2396, 2540, 2541, 2545, 2551). The word is conjunctive of heaven and earth (n. 2310, 2495, 9212, 9216, 9357, 10,357). The word therefore is written by mere correspondences (n. 1404, 1408, 1409, 1540, 1619, 1659, 1709, 1783, 8615, 10,687). In the inmost sense of the word the Lord alone and His Kingdom are treated of (n. 1873, 2249, 2523, 7014, 9357).

[4] The word in the sense of the letter is natural (n. 8783). By reason that what is natural is the ultimate, wherein spiritual and celestial things close, and on which they subsist as on their foundation, and that otherwise the internal or spiritual sense of the word without the external or

is the First and the Last thereof, therefore, that all things might exist according to order, He was willing to be born on this earth, and be made the Word, according to what is written in *John*:

> In the beginning was the Word, and the Word was with God, and God was the Word. This was in the beginning with God. All things were made by Him, and without Him was not anything made which was made. *And the Word became flesh, and dwelt among us, and we beheld His glory, the glory as of the Only-begotten of the Father.* No one has seen God at any time; the Only-begotten Son, who is in the bosom of the Father, He hath brought Him forth to view (i. 1-14, 18). The Word is the Lord as to the Divine truth, thus the Divine truth from the Lord.[5] But this is an arcanum which falls within the understanding of only a few.

---

natural sense, would be as a house without a foundation (n. 9430, 9433, 9824, 10,044, 10,136).

[5] The Word is the Lord as to the Divine truth, thus the Divine truth from the Lord (n. 2859, 4692, 5075, 9987). By the Divine truth all things were created and made (n. 2803, 2884, 5272, 7835).

NINE

The Earths
in the Starry Heaven

123 THEY WHO ARE IN HEAVEN CAN SPEAK AND CONVERSE with angels and spirits who are not only from the earths in this solar system, but also with those who are from other earths in the universe out of this system; and not only with the spirits and angels there, but also with the inhabitants themselves, but only with those whose interiors are open, so that they can hear such as speak from heaven. The same is the case with man during his abode in the world, to whom it has been granted by the Lord to speak with spirits and angels. For man is a spirit as to his interiors, the body which he carries about in the world only serving him for performing functions in this natural or terrestrial sphere, which is the ultimate, But it is granted to no one to speak as a spirit with angels and spirits, unless he be such that he can consociate with angels as to faith and love; nor can he so consociate, unless he have faith and love to the Lord; for man is joined to the Lord by faith and love to Him, that is, by truths of doctrine and goods of life from Him; and when he is conjoined to the Lord, he is secure from the assaults of evil spirits from hell. With others the interiors cannot be so far opened, since they are not in the

Lord. This is the reason why there are few at this day to whom it is granted to speak and converse with angels; a manifest proof whereof is, that the existence of spirits and angels is scarcely believed at this day, much less that they are with every man, and that by them man has connection with heaven, and through heaven with the Lord. Still less is it believed that man, when he dies as to the body, lives a spirit, even in a human form as before.

124 Because at this day with many in the church there is no belief in the life after death, and scarce any belief in heaven, nor in the Lord as the God of heaven and earth; therefore the interiors which are of my spirit have been opened by the Lord, so that while still in the body, I can at the same time be with angels in heaven, and not only speak with them, but also see the stupendous things there, and describe them; so that it may not chance to be said hereafter, "Who has come to us from heaven and told us that there is such a place, and what there is there?" But I know that they who in heart have before denied heaven and hell and the life after death, will still confirm themselves against them, and deny them; for it is easier to make a crow white, than to make those believe who have once rejected faith in the heart. The reason is, that they always think of such things from the negative, and not from the affirmative. Nevertheless, let what has been said hitherto, and what is still further to be said concerning angels and spirits, be for the few who are in faith. And that the rest also may be led along to something of acknowledgment it has been conceded to relate such things as delight and attract the man who is desirous of knowing; and now about the earths in the starry heaven.

125 He who does not know the arcana of heaven, cannot believe that a man can see earths so distant, and relate anything about them from the experiences of the senses. But let him know that the spaces and distances, and thence the progressions in the natural world, are, in their origin and first cause, changes of the state of the interiors, and with angels and spirits appear according to these changes;[1] and that thus they can by these changes be apparently transferred from

---

[1] Movements, progressions, and changes of place in the other life are changes of state of the interiors of the life, and still they appear to spirits and angels as real changes of place (n. 1273-1277, 1377, 3356, 5605, 10,734).

one place to another, and from one earth to another, even to the earths which are at the end of the universe. So also may a man be transferred as to his spirit, his body still remaining in its place. Thus it has been done with me, since by the Divine mercy of the Lord it has been given me to have intercourse with spirits as a spirit, and at the same time with men as a man. That a man can be so transferred as to his spirit, the sensual man cannot understand, since he is in space and time, and measures his movements according to them.

126 That there are many worlds, may be evident to every one, from there being so many constellations visible in the universe; and it is known in the learned world that every fixed star is like a sun in its place; for it remains fixed like the sun of our earth in its place; and that the distance makes it appear small in form like a star. Consequently that like the sun of our world, it has round it planets, which are earths; and the reason that these do not appear to our eyes, is their being at such an immense distance, and having only the light of their star, which cannot be reflected again as far as here. For what other purpose is there so great a heaven with so many stars? For the end of the creation of the universe is man, that from man there may be an angelic heaven. What would the human race, and thence an angelic heaven, from one earth, be for the Infinite Creator, for Whom a thousand earths, nay, tens of thousands, would not be enough? By calculation it appears that if there were a million earths in the universe, and men on every earth to the number of three hundred millions, and two hundred generations in six thousand years, and if to each man or spirit were given the space of three cubic ells, the whole number of so many men or spirits, collected into one body, would still not fill the space of the thousandth part of this earth, thus perhaps not more than the space of a single satellite around the planet Jupiter or Saturn; which would be a space scarce discernible in the universe, for a satellite is hardly visible to the naked eye. What is this to the Creator of the universe? to Whom there would not be enough if the whole universe should be filled, for He is Infinite. On these matters I have spoken with angels, who said that they have a similar idea of the fewness of the human race in comparison with the infinity of the Creator, although they do not think from spaces, but from states; and that according to their idea, earths to the number of as many myriads as could be conceived by thought, would still be as nothing at all to the Lord. But in what now follows, the earths in the starry heavens shall be described from experience itself; from which it will also be evident how I was transferred thither as to my spirit, my body remaining in its place.

TEN

☼

The First Earth
in the Starry Heaven

127 I WAS LED BY THE LORD BY MEANS OF ANGELS TO A certain earth in the starry heaven, where it was given me to look into the earth itself, yet not to speak with the inhabitants there, but with the spirits who were from it. All the inhabitants or men of every earth, after the life in the world is finished, become spirits, and remain near their own earth. From these spirits, however, information is given about their earth, and about the state of the inhabitants there; for men who leave the body bring with them all their former life, and all their memory.[1] To be led to earths in the universe is not to be led and transferred thither as to the body, but as to the spirit; and the spirit is led by variations of the state of the interior life, which appear to it as progressions through space.[2] Approaches also are made according to agreements or similarities of states of life; for agreement or similarity of life conjoins, disagreement and dissimilarity disjoin. From this may be evident how trans-

---

[1] Man after death retains the memory of all his affairs in the world (n. 2476-2486).
[2] Movements, progressions, and changes of place in the other life are changes of state of the interiors of the life, and still they appear to spirits and angels as real changes of place (n. 1273-1277, 1377, 3356, 5605, 10,734).

ference is made as to the spirit, and approach to what is distant, the man still remaining in his place. But to lead the spirit beyond its own world by variations of the state of its interiors, and to make the variations advance successively even to a state agreeing with or similar to that of those to whom it is led, is in the power of the Lord alone. For there must be continual direction and foresight from first to last, in going and returning; especially with a man who is still in the world of nature as to the body, and thereby in space. That this has been done, those who are in the bodily senses and think from them, cannot be induced to believe, for the reason that what is of bodily sense cannot comprehend progressions without space. But still they who think from the sense of their spirit, somewhat removed or withdrawn from the sense of the body, thus interiorly in themselves, may be led to believe and to comprehend; since in the idea of the interior thought there is not space nor time, but instead thereof those things from which spaces and times exist. It is for such persons that what follows concerning the earths in the starry heaven is related, and not for others, unless they will suffer themselves to be instructed.

128 In a state of wakefulness I was led as to the spirit by the Lord, by means of angels, to a certain earth in the universe, accompanied by some spirits from this world. Our progress was made toward the right, and lasted two hours. Near the limit of our solar system, there appeared at first a shining bright cloud, but dense, and beyond it a fiery smoke ascending out of a great chasm. It was a vast gulf separating our solar world on that side from some worlds of the starry heavens. That fiery smoke appeared at a considerable distance. I was borne across the middle of it; and then there appeared beneath in that chasm or gulf very many men, who were spirits; for spirits all appear in the human form, and actually are men. I also heard them speaking with one another; but whence they were and their quality was not given me to know. Yet one of them said to me that they were guards, lest spirits should pass from this world into another in the universe without leave having been given. That it was so, was also confirmed; for some spirits who were in our company, but had not received the ability to pass over, when they came to that great inter-space, began to cry out vehemently that they were perishing; for they were like those who are struggling in agony with death, and therefore they stopped on that side of the gulf, nor could they be taken any further, as the fiery smoke that exhaled from the gulf enveloped them and thus tortured them.

129 Afterwards I was carried along through that great chasm, and at length I arrived at a place where I stopped; and there then appeared to me spirits overhead with whom it was given me to speak. From their speech, and from their genius of apprehending and explaining things, I clearly perceived that they were from another earth for they were quite different from the spirits of our solar system. They also perceived from my speech that I was from afar.

130 After we had spoken for sometime on various matters, I asked what God they worshiped. They said they worshiped an angel, who appears to them as a Divine Man, shining with light; and that He instructs them and gives them to perceive what they ought to do. They said further that they know that the Most High God is in the sun of the angelic heaven; and that He appears to their angel, and not to themselves; and that He is too great for them to dare to adore Him. The angel whom they worshiped was an angelic society, to which it was given by the Lord to preside over them, and to teach the way of what is just and right. They therefore have light from a certain flame, which appears like a small torch, quite fiery and yellow. The reason is because they do not adore the Lord, and thus they do not have light from the sun of the angelic heaven, but from an angelic society. For an angelic society, when it is given by the Lord, can present such light to the spirits who are in a lower region. That angelic society was also seen by me, high above them; and there was also seen there the flamy appearance from which their light came.

131 As to the rest, they were modest, and somewhat simple, but yet they thought very well. From the light with them it might be concluded what their intellectual faculty is; for the understanding is according to the reception of the light which is in the heavens; since the Divine truth proceeding from the Lord as a sun is what shines there, and enables the angels not only to see, but also to understand.[3]

132 I was instructed that the inhabitants and spirits of that earth have reference in the Greatest Man to something in the spleen, of which I was confirmed by an influx into the spleen when they were speaking with me.

133 They were asked about the sun of their system, which illumines their earth. They said that the sun there appears flamy; and when I represented the size of the sun of our earth, they said that theirs is smaller; for their sun to our eyes is a star, and I was told by angels that it is among the smaller stars. They also said that the starry heaven is likewise seen from their earth, and that a star larger than the rest appears to them toward the west. I was told from heaven that this is our sun.

134 Presently my sight was opened, so that I could look somewhat into that earth itself; and there appeared many meadows and woods with leafy trees, and also woolly sheep. I afterward saw some of the inhabitants, who were of the lower class, clothed in a dress much like that of peasants in Europe. There was also seen a man with his woman. She appeared of handsome figure and graceful carriage, and the man likewise. But, what I wondered at, he had a pompous gait, with a rather haughty step; while the woman, on the contrary, walked with a humble step. It was said by the angels that such is the custom on that earth, and that the men who are such are loved, because nevertheless they are good. I was further told that it is not permitted them to have many wives, because it is contrary to their laws. The woman whom I saw had before her breast a broad garment, with which she could screen herself, while it was so made that she could insert her arms and wrap it about herself, and so walk away. The lower part of it could be drawn up, and when drawn up and applied

---

[3] The light in the heavens is great (n. 1117, 1521, 1522, 1533, 1619-1632, 4527, 5400, 8644). All the light in the heavens is from the Lord as a sun there (n. 1053, 1521, 3195, 3341, 3636, 4415, 9548, 9684, 10,809). Divine truth proceeding from the Lord appears in the heavens as light (n. 3195, 3222, 5400, 8644, 9399, 9548, 9684). That light illumines both the sight and the understanding of angels and spirits (n. 2776, 3138). The light of heaven also illumines the understanding of man (n. 1524, 3138, 3167, 4408, 6608, 8707, 9128, 9399, 10,569).

to the body, it appeared like an upper garment covering the chest, such as is worn by the women of our earth. But the same garment served also for the man, who was seen to take it from the woman and apply it to his back, loosening the lower part, which then flowed down to his feet, like a toga, and thus clothed he walked about. What I saw on that earth, was not seen with the eyes of my body, but with the eyes of my spirit; and the spirit can see the things that are on an earth, when it is granted by the Lord.

135 Since I know that it will be doubted whether it is in any way possible for a man to see with the eyes of his spirit anything on an earth so distant, it is allowed me to say how this thing is. Distances in the other life are not like distances on earth. In the other life distances are altogether according to the states of the interiors of any one. Those who are in a like state, are together in one society and in one place. Everything is present there according to similarity of state and everything is distant according to dissimilarity of state. Hence it was that I was near that earth when I was led by the Lord into a state similar to that of its spirits and inhabitants, and that being then present I spoke with them. From this it is plain that the earths in the spiritual world are not distant in the same way as in the natural world; but only apparently, according to the states of life of the inhabitants and spirits there. The state of life is the state of affections as to love and faith. In regard to a spirit being able to see the things which are on an earth, or what is the same, a man as to his spirit, it is allowed me to explain how this also is. Neither spirits nor angels can, by their own sight, see anything that is in the world; for to them the light of the world, or of the sun, is as dense thick darkness, just as man by his bodily sight cannot see anything that is in the other life; for to him the light of heaven is as dense thick darkness. But still, spirits and angels, when it is the Lord's good pleasure, can see the things that are in the world through the eyes of man. But this the Lord does not grant to any others than those whom He gives to speak with spirits and angels, and to be together with them. Through my eyes it has been given them to see the things which are in the world, and as plainly as I did; and also to hear men speaking with me. It has sometimes happened, that some through me have seen their friends whom they had in the life of the body, just at present as before, and they were astounded. They have also seen their husbands, or wives, and their children, and wished to tell them that they were present and saw them, and also wanted me to tell them about their state in the other life. But I was prohibited from telling them and revealing to them that they were thus seen, even for the reason that they would have called me insane, or would have thought that it was delirium of mind. For it was known to me, that although they acknowledged with the lips, still they did not believe in the heart, that there were spirits, and that the dead had risen and were among spirits, and that these could see and hear through a man. When my interior sight was first opened, and those who were in the other life saw through my eyes the world and the things that were in it, they were so astonished that they called this the miracle of miracles, and were affected with a new joy, that thus there was granted a communication of earth with heaven, and of heaven with earth. This joy lasted for months; but afterwards it became familiar. Now they have ceased to wonder. I have been instructed that the spirits and angels with other men, see nothing at all of what is in the world, but only perceive the thoughts and affections of those with whom they are. From this it may be evident that man was so created, that while living in the world among men, he might at the same time also live in heaven among angels, and the converse; thus that heaven and the world with a man might be together, and act as one; and that men might know what is in heaven, and angels what is in the world; and when men die, they might thus pass out of the Lord's kingdom on earth into the Lord's kingdom in heaven, not as into a different kingdom, but as into the same in which they also were when they lived in the body. But because man has become so corporeal, he has closed heaven to himself.

136 Lastly I spoke with the spirits who were from that earth about various things on our earth, especially about there being sciences here which are not elsewhere, as astronomy, geometry, mechanics, physics, chemistry, medicine, optics, philosophy: and also arts, which are not known elsewhere, as those of ship-building, of casting metals, of writing upon paper, and of printing what is written by types, and so of communicating it to others on the earth, and also of preserving it for posterity for thousands of years; as I told them had been done with the Word which is from the Lord; and therefore there is a permanent Revelation on our earth.

137 Lastly was shown me the hell of those who are from that earth. Those who were seen from it terrified one most exceedingly, and I dare not describe their monstrous faces. There were also seen there enchantresses, who practice direful arts. These appeared clothed in green, and they struck me with horror.

ELEVEN

The Second Earth
in the Starry Heaven

138 I WAS AFTERWARDS LED BY THE LORD TO AN EARTH in the universe which was further distant from our earth than the foregoing of which we have been just speaking. That it was further distant was plain from this, that I was two days in being led thither as to my spirit. This earth was to the left, whereas the former was to the right. Inasmuch as remoteness in the spiritual world does not arise from distance of place, but from difference of state, as was said above, therefore from the slowness of my progression thither, which lasted two days, I might conclude that the state of the interiors with them, which is the state of the affections and thence of the thoughts, differed proportionately from the state of the interiors with spirits from our earth. Being conveyed thither as to the spirit by changes of the state of the interiors, I was enabled to observe the successive changes themselves before I arrived thither. This was done whilst I was awake.

139 When I arrived thither, the earth was not seen, but only the spirits who were from that earth; for, as also was said above, the spirits of every earth appear about their own earth, by reason that they

84

are of a genius similar to that of the inhabitants, for they are from them, and in order that they may serve them. Those spirits were seen at a considerable height above my head whence they observed me as I approached. It is to be known that they who stand on high in the other life can look at those who are beneath them, and the higher they are the greater is the extent of their vision; and they can not only look at them, but likewise can speak with them. From their state of elevation they observed that I was not from their earth, but from another afar off; wherefore they addressed me inquiring concerning various things, to which it was given me to reply; and among other things I related to them from what earth I was, and what kind of earth it was. Afterwards I spoke to them concerning the other earths in our solar system; and at the same time also concerning the spirits of the earth or planet Mercury, that they wander about to many earths for the purpose of procuring for themselves knowledges of various matters. On hearing this, they said that they had likewise seen those spirits with them.

140 It was told me by the angels from our earth, that the inhabitants and spirits of that earth have reference in the Greatest Man to *keenness of vision,* and for this reason they appear on high, and that they are also exceedingly clear-sighted. Because they had reference to that, and because they saw very clearly what was beneath them, in talking with them I also compared them to eagles, which fly on high, and have a clear and wide vision around them. But at this they were indignant, supposing that I believed them to be like eagles as to rapine, and thus that they were evil. But I replied that I did not liken them to eagles as to rapine, but as to keenness of sight.

141 They were asked about the God whom they worshiped; and they answered that they worshiped God visible and invisible, God visible under the Human form, and God invisible not under any form; and it was found from their speech, and also from the ideas of their thought as communicated to me, that the visible God was our Lord Himself, and they also called Him Lord. To this it was given to reply, that on our earth also God is worshiped as invisible and as visible; and that God invisible is called the Father, and visible the Lord, but that the two are one, as He Himself taught, saying that no man hath ever seen the form of the Father, but that the Father and He are one; and that He who sees Him sees the Father; and that the Father is in Him, and He in the Father; consequently that the two are the Divine in one Person. That these are the words of the Lord Himself, may be seen in *John* (5:37; 10:30; 14:7, 9-11).

142 After a while I saw other spirits from the same earth, who appeared in a place below the former, with whom also I spoke. But they were idolaters, for they worshiped an idol of stone, resembling a man, but not beautiful. It is to be known that all who come into the other life have at first a worship like their worship in the world, but that they are gradually withdrawn from it. The reason is, that all worship remains implanted in man's interior life, from which it cannot be removed and eradicated but by degrees. On seeing this, it was given me to tell them that they ought not to worship what is dead, but what is living; to which they answered that they know that God lives, and that a stone does not; but that they think of the living God when they look upon a stone in the form of a man; and that otherwise the ideas of their thought cannot be fixed and determined to the invisible God. Then it was given me to tell them that the ideas of thought can be fixed and determined to the invisible God when they are fixed and determined to the Lord, Who is God visible in thought under the Human form; and thus that man can be conjoined to the invisible God in thought and affection, consequently in faith and love, when he is conjoined to the Lord, but in no other way.

143 The spirits who were seen on high were asked whether on their earth they live under the rule of princes and kings; to which they answered that they do not know what such rule is; and that they live under themselves, distinguished into nations, families, and houses. They were asked whether they are secure in this way. They said that they are, since one family does not envy another, nor wish to take anything away from it. They were indignant at being asked such questions, which seemed to imply that there was hostility among them, or need of protection against robbers. What more is needed, they said, than to have food and clothing, and so to dwell contented and quiet under themselves.

144 Being questioned further about their earth, they said that they have meadows, flower gardens, woods full of fruit trees, and also lakes in which are fish; and that they have birds of a blue color with golden wings, and animals of various sizes. Among the smaller they mentioned one kind which had the back humped, like the camels on our earth. They do not, however, eat the flesh of these animals, but only the flesh of fishes, and also the fruits of trees and leguminous plants of the earth. They said further that they do not dwell in built houses, but in groves, in which they make a shelter for themselves among the foliage against rain and the heat of the sun.

145 They were asked about their sun, which is seen as a star from our earth, and they said that it appears fiery; not larger to the sight than a man's head. I was told by angels that the star which is their sun is among the smaller stars, not far distant from the celestial equator.

146 Spirits were seen, in a similar appearance to what they had when they were men on their earth. They had a face not unlike that of the men of our earth, except that the eyes and nose were smaller. As this seemed to me somewhat of a deformity, they said that to them small eyes and a small nose are marks of beauty. A woman was seen, dressed in a gown on which were roses of various colors. I inquired of what materials they make their garments on that earth. They answered that from plants they gather such things as they can spin into threads, and that they then lay the threads side by side in double and triple layers, and moisten them with a glutinous liquid, and so give it consistency, coloring it afterward with juices from herbs. I was likewise shown how they prepare the threads: they sit leaning back on a seat, and twist the thread with the toes; and when it is twisted, they draw it to them, and finish it with the hands.

147 They also said that on that earth a husband has only one wife, and not more, and that they have from ten to fifteen children. They added that harlots are also found there; but that after the life of the body, when they become spirits, they are sorceresses, and are cast into hell.

TWELVE

A Third Earth
in the Starry Heaven

148 SOME SPIRITS APPEARED AT A DISTANCE WHO WERE not willing to come near. The reason was that they could not be with the spirits of our earth who were then around me. From this I perceived that they were from another earth, and afterward I was told that they were from a certain earth in the universe; but where that earth is, I was not informed. These spirits were altogether unwilling to think of their body, and indeed of anything corporeal and material, differently from the spirits from our earth. This was why they were not willing to come near. But still after the removal of some of the spirits of our earth, they came nearer and spoke with me. But then anxiety was felt, arising from the collision of spheres; for spiritual spheres encompass all spirits and societies of spirits; and because they flow forth from the life of the affections and of the thoughts therefrom, therefore where there are opposing affections there arises collision, and thence anxiety. The spirits of our earth said that they did not dare to approach them, since when they were approaching, they not only were seized with anxiety, but also appeared to themselves as if bound hand and foot with serpents,

88

from which they could not be loosed until they withdrew. This appearance had its origin from correspondence; for the spirits of our earth have reference in the Greatest Man to the external sense, thus to the corporeal sensual, and this sensual is represented in the other life by serpents.[1]

149 Because the nature of the spirits of that earth is such, they appear before the eyes of other spirits, not like others, in a manifest human form, but like clouds, and for the most part like a dark cloud, in which is mingled something of a bright human appearance. But they said that they are white within, and that when they become angels, the dark color is turned into a beautiful blue, as was also shown to me. I asked whether they had such an idea of their body, when they lived as men in the world. They said that the men of their earth make no account of their bodies, but only of the spirit in the body, because they know that this is to live to eternity, but the body to perish. They also said that many on their earth believe that the spirit of the body has been from eternity, and was infused into the body at conception. But they added that they now know it is not so, and that they repent having been in such a false opinion.

150 When I asked whether they wished to see anything on our earth, and said that this could be done through my eyes (see above n. 135), they answered at first that they could not, and then that they did not wish it; since they would see only earthly and material things, from which they remove their thoughts as far as possible. But still there were represented before them magnificent palaces, like those of kings and princes on our earth, for such things can be represented before spirits, and when represented, they appear altogether as if they were there. But the spirits from that earth set no value upon them, calling them marble images; and then they told me that they had more magnificent ones, which are their sanctuaries, not of stone, but of wood. When it was said to them that these were still earthly, they answered that they were not, but heavenly; because when they

---

[1] Man's external sensual is represented in the spiritual world by serpents, because it is in the lowest things, and in comparison with the interiors with man, lies on the ground and as it were creeps; and that they were thence called serpents, who reasoned from that sensual (n. 195-197, 6398, 6949).

look upon them, they have not an earthly, but a heavenly idea, believing that they will also see similar ones in heaven after death.

151 They then represented their sanctuaries before the spirits of our earth, who said that they had seen nothing more magnificent; and as I also saw them, I can therefore describe them. They are constructed of trees, not cut down, but growing in their native soil. They said that on their earth there were trees of wonderful growth and height. These from their beginnings they arrange in order, so that they serve for porticos and walks, and by cutting and pruning the branches when they are tender, they fit and prepare them so that while they are growing they may intertwine and unite to make the base and floor of the sanctuary, and rise on the sides for the walls, and bend above into arches for the roof. By these means they construct the sanctuary with admirable art, elevated high above the earth, and they also prepare an ascent into it by successive branches of the trees extending out and firmly connected. Moreover they adorn the sanctuary without and within in various ways, by bending the leafy bows into various forms. Thus they build entire groves. But what these sanctuaries are within, I was not permitted to see. It was only told me that the light of their sun is let into them through apertures between the branches, and is here and there transmitted through crystals, by which the light falling on the walls is variegated into colors like the rainbow, especially the colors blue and orange, which they love more than the rest. Such is their architecture, which they prefer to the most magnificent palaces of our earth.

152 They said, further, that the inhabitants do not live in high places, but on the earth in low cottages, for the reason that high places are for the Lord, who is in heaven, and low places for men, who are on earth. Their cottages were also shown to me. They were oblong, having within along the walls a continuous couch, on which they lie one after another. On the side opposite the door is a semicircular recess, before which is a table, and behind this a fireplace, by which the whole room is lighted. In the fireplace there is not a burning fire, but luminous wood which gives out as much light as the flame of a wood fire. They said that those pieces of wood appear in the evening like a fire of burning coals.

153 They said that they do not live in societies, but each house is by itself; and that they are societies when they meet for worship, and that then those who teach walk below the sanctuary, and the rest in the porticos at the sides; and that in those meetings they have interior joys, from the sight of the sanctuary, and from the worship therein.

154 Respecting Divine worship they said that they acknowledge God under the Human form, thus our Lord; for whoever acknowledge the God of the universe under the Human form, are accepted by our Lord and led by Him. The rest cannot be led, because they think without a form. They added that the inhabitants of their earth are instructed in the things of heaven by a kind of immediate intercourse with angels and spirits, into which they can be led by the Lord more easily than others, because they reject what is corporeal from their thought and affection. I asked what becomes of those among them who are evil. They said that on their earth it is not permitted to be wicked; but that if any one thinks and does evil, he is reproved by a certain spirit, who threatens death to him if he persists in so doing; and that when he persists, he dies in a swoon; and that in this way the men of that earth are preserved from the contamination of the evil. One such spirit was also sent to me, and spoke with me as he did with his own people. Moreover he brought something of pain to the region of my abdomen, saying that thus he does to those who think and do evil, and threatens death to them, if they persist. They said that those who profane holy things are severely punished; and that before the punishing spirit comes there appear to them in vision the jaws of a lion, wide open, of a livid color, which seems as if it would swallow their head, and tear it from the body, whereby they are seized with horror. They call the punishing spirit the devil.

155 As they desired to know how it is with regard to revelation on our earth, I said that it is effected by writing and by preaching from the Word, and not by immediate intercourse with spirits and angels; and that what is written can be printed and published, and be read and comprehended by entire communities, and thus the life may be amended. They wondered greatly that such an art, entirely unknown elsewhere, should exist here. But they comprehended that on this earth, where corporeal and earthly things are so much loved, Divine things from heaven cannot flow in and be received in any other way; and that it would be dangerous for them to speak with angels.

156 The spirits of that earth appear above in the plane of the head, toward the right. All spirits are distinguished by their situation with respect to the human body; and this for the reason that the whole heaven corresponds to all things of man.[2] These spirits keep themselves in that plane and at that distance because their correspondence is not with the externals in man, but with the interiors. Their action is into the left knee, above and a little below, with a certain very sensible vibration; which is a sign that they correspond to *the conjunction of natural and heavenly things.*

---

[2] Heaven corresponds to the Lord, and man as to each and all things corresponds to heaven, and hence heaven, before the Lord, is a man in a large effigy, and may be called the Greatest Man (n. 2996, 2998, 3624-3649, 3636-3643, 3741-3745, 4625) Concerning the correspondence of man, and of all things pertaining to him, with the Greatest Man, which is heaven, in general, from experience (n. 3021, 3624-3649, 3741-3751, 3883-3896, 4039-4051, 4215-4228, 4318-4331, 4403-4421, 4527-4533, 4622-4633, 4652-4660, 4791-4805, 4931-4953, 5050-5061, 5171-5189, 5377-5396, 5552-5573, 5711-5727, 10,030).

THIRTEEN

A Fourth Earth in the Starry Heaven

157 I WAS CONDUCTED TO STILL ANOTHER EARTH IN THE universe beyond our solar system, which was effected by changes of the state of my mind, and thus as to the spirit. For, as has been sometimes said before, the spirit is conducted from place to place in no other way than by changes of the state of its interiors, which changes appear to it altogether like movements from place to place, or like journeyings. These changes lasted continuously for about ten hours, before from the state of my life I arrived at the state of their life; thus before I was brought thither as to my spirit. I was borne toward the east to the left, and I seemed to be sensibly elevated above the plane of the horizon. It was also given me to observe very clearly the progression and advance from the place where I had been before, until at length those from whom I departed were no longer in sight. Meanwhile I spoke on various subjects with the spirits who went with me. A certain spirit was also with us, who when he lived in the world had been a primate and a preacher, and likewise a very pathetic writer. From my idea of him the accompanying spirits supposed that in heart he must be eminently a Christian. For in the

world an idea is received and a judgment formed from one's preaching and writings, and not from his life, unless this is conspicuous; and if there appears anything inconsistent in his life, still it is excused; for the idea, or the thought and perception concerning any one, draws everything to its own side.

158 After I had observed that as to my spirit I was in the starry heaven far beyond the world of our sun, for this might be observed from the changes of state and from the apparent continual progression thence, which lasted nearly ten hours, I at length heard spirits speaking near some earth, which was afterward also seen by me. When I came near to them, after some conversation, they said that visitors sometimes come to them from elsewhere, who speak with them about God and confuse the ideas of their thought. They also showed the way by which they come, from which it was perceived that they were of the spirits from our earth. Being then asked wherein their thoughts were confused, they answered that it was by those spirits saying that one must believe in the Divine as distinguished into three Persons, which they still call one God. And when they examine the idea of their thoughts, it is presented as a trine not continuous, but discrete; and with some, as three persons speaking together one to another; and with some, as two seated together, and a third hearkening to them, and then going from them; and though they call each Person God, and have a different idea concerning each, they still call them one God. They complained exceedingly that they confuse them by thinking three and saying one, when yet one ought to think as he speaks, and speak as he thinks. The spirit who in the world had been a primate and a preacher, and was with me, was then examined as to what idea he had concerning one God and three Persons. He represented three Gods, but these as one by continuity, but he presented this trinal one as invisible because Divine; and when he presented this, it was perceived that he then thought only of the Father, and not of the Lord; and that his idea of the invisible God was no other than as of nature in its firsts; from which it resulted that to him the inmost of nature was his Divine, and thus that from this he could be easily led to acknowledge nature as God. It is to be known that in the other life the idea of any one upon any subject is presented to the life; and that by this means every one is explored as to what thought and perception he has concerning matters of faith; and that the idea of the thought concerning God is the chief of them all; for by that, if it is genuine, conjunction is effected with the Divine, and thence with heaven. Being then asked what idea they had of God, these spirits answered that they did not conceive of God as invisible, but as visible under the Human form; and that they know this not only from interior perception, but also from His appearing to them as a Man; adding that if according to the idea of some visitors they should conceive of God as invisible, thus without form and quality, they could not think at all of God, since what is thus invisible does not fall into any idea of thought. On hearing this, it was given me to say to them that they do well to think of God under the Human form; and that many from our earth think in like manner, especially when they think of the Lord; and that the ancients thought in no other way. I then told them about Abraham, Lot, Gideon, and Manoah and his wife, and what is related of them in our Word, namely, that they saw God under the Human form and acknowledged Him thus seen as the Creator of the universe, and called Him Jehovah, and this also from interior perception; but that at this day that interior perception has perished in the Christian world, and only remains with the simple who are in faith.

159 Before this was said, they believed that our company also was of those who wished to confuse them by the idea of three concerning God. When therefore they heard these things, they were affected with joy, and said that some were also sent to them by God, whom they then called the Lord, who teach them concerning Him; and that they were not willing to admit visitors who disturb them, especially by the idea of three Persons in the Divinity, since they know that God is one, consequently that the Divine is one, and not a unanimity of three, unless they would think of God as of an angel, in whom the inmost of life is something invisible, from which he thinks and is wise, and the external of life what is visible under the human form, from which he sees and acts, and the proceeding of life that which is the sphere of love and faith from him, for from every spirit and angel proceeds a sphere of life by which he is known at a distance; and as to the Lord, that the proceeding of life from Him is the Divine Itself which fills and constitutes the heavens, because it proceeds from the *esse* itself of the life of love and faith. They said that in this and in no other way could they perceive a Trine and a One at the same time. On hearing this, it was given me to say that such an idea of a Trine and a One together agrees with the angelic idea of the Lord; and that it is from the Lord's own teaching concerning Himself; for He teaches that the Father and He are one; that the Father is in Him, and He in the Father; that whoso sees Him, sees the Father; and that He who believes in Him, believes in the Father and knows Him; also that the Comforter, by whom is meant the proceeding Divine, and whom He calls the Spirit of truth, as also the Holy Spirit, proceeds from Him, and speaks not from Himself, but from Him. Moreover, that the idea of a Trine and of One at the same time agrees with the *esse* and *existere* of the Lord's life, when He was in the world. The *esse* of His life was the Divine Itself, for He was conceived of Jehovah, and the *esse* of any one's life is that from which he is conceived; the *existere* of life from that *esse* is the Human in form. The *esse* of every man's life which he has from his father, is called the soul; and the *existere* of life therefrom is called the body. The soul and the body constitute one man. The likeness between both is like that between that which is in effort and that which is in the act thence, for the act is the effort acting, and so the two are one. Effort in man is called the will, and effort acting is called action. The body is the instrument, by which the will, which is the principal, acts; and the instrument and the principal in acting are one; thus the soul and the body are one. The angels in heaven have such an idea concerning the soul and the body; and thus they know that the Lord made His Human Divine from the Divine in Himself, which He had as His soul from the Father. The faith also received everywhere in the Christian world does not dissent from this, for it teaches: "Although Christ is God and Man, yet He is not two, but one Christ; yea, He is altogether a one and only Person; for as the body and the soul are one man, so also God and Man is one Christ."[1] Because there was such a union, or such a One in the Lord, He therefore, otherwise than

---

[1] From the Athanasian Creed.

any man, rose not only as to the soul, but also as to the body, which
He glorified in the world; concerning which He also instructed
His disciples, saying:

> Handle Me and see; for a spirit hath not flesh and bones,
> as ye see Me have.[2]

These things those spirits well understood, for such things fall into
the understanding of angelic spirits. They then added that the Lord
alone has power in the heavens, and that the heavens are His. To
which it was given me to respond that the church on our earth also
knows this, from the mouth of the Lord Himself, before He ascended
into heaven; for He then said:

> All power is given unto Me in heaven and in earth.

160 I afterward spoke with those spirits concerning their earth;
for all spirits know about their earth when their natural or external
memory is opened by the Lord; since they have this with them from
the world, but it is not opened except by the good pleasure of the
Lord. The spirits then said respecting their earth from which they
were, that when leave is given them, they appear to the inhabitants
of their earth, and speak with them as men; and that this is done by
their being let into their natural or external memory, and thus into
such thought as they were in when they lived in the world; and that
the inhabitants then have their interior sight, or the sight of their
spirit, opened, from which they see them. They added that the inhabitants do not know that they are not men of their earth, and first
perceive that they are not, when they are suddenly taken away from
their sight. I told them that such was the case on our earth in ancient times, as with Abraham, Sarah, Lot, the inhabitants of Sodom,
Manoah and his wife, Joshua, Mary, Elizabeth, and the prophets in
general; and that the Lord appeared in like manner, and those who
saw Him did not know otherwise than that He was a man of the
earth, before He revealed Himself. But that this is rarely done at this
day, lest by such things men should be compelled to believe; for a

---

[2] Man rises again as to his spirit immediately after death, and he is the human form, and
that as to each and every particular he is a man (n. 4527, 5006, 5078, 8939, 8991, 10,594, 10,597,
10,758). Man rises again only as to his spirit, and not as to his body (n. 10,593, 10,594). The Lord
alone rose again as to the body also (n. 1729, 2083, 5078, 10,825).

compelled faith, such as is that which enters through miracles, does not remain fixed, and would also be hurtful to those with whom faith might be implanted through the Word in a state not compelled.

161 The spirit who in the world had been a primate and a preacher, did not at all believe that there were any other earths than ours, because he had thought in the world that the Lord was born on this earth only, and that no one has salvation without the Lord. He was therefore reduced to such a state as the spirits are reduced when they appear on their earth as men (see just above), and thus was sent to that earth, so as not only to see it, but also to speak with its inhabitants. When this was done, communication was also thereby granted me, so that I in like manner saw the inhabitants, and some things also upon that earth (see above, n. 135). There then appeared four kinds of men, but one kind after another in succession. First were seen men clothed; next men naked of the color of human flesh; afterward men naked, but with bodies inflamed; and lastly black men.

162 When the spirit who had been a primate and a preacher was with those who were clothed, there appeared a woman of a very beautiful face, dressed in a simple garment, with a tunic that hung gracefully behind her and was brought up over the arms. She had a beautiful headdress, in the form of a chaplet of flowers. That spirit was greatly delighted at the sight of this virgin, and spoke with her, and also took her hand. But as she perceived that he was a spirit, and not of that earth, she hurried away from him. There afterward appeared to him on the right many other women, who were tending sheep and lambs, which they were then leading to a watering trough that was supplied with water by a small ditch from a lake. They were similarly clothed, and held shepherds' crooks in their hands, by which they guided the sheep and lambs to drink. They said that the sheep went in the way to which they pointed with their crooks. The sheep seen were large, with woolly tails, both broad and long. The faces of the women when seen nearer were full and beautiful. The men were also seen, and their faces were of the color of human flesh, as on our earth; but with the difference, that the lower part of the face, in place of a beard, was black, and the nose more the color of snow than of flesh. Afterward the spirit above mentioned, who had been a preacher in the world, was led on further, but unwillingly, because his thought was still on that woman with whom he was delighted, as was made manifest by somewhat of a shadow from him still appearing in the former place. He then came to those who were naked, and who were seen walking together two and two, being husband and wife, girded with a covering about the loins and a certain covering upon the head. That spirit when with them was led into that state in which he was in the world when he wished to preach, and said that he would preach to them the Lord crucified. But they said that they were not willing to hear any such thing, because they did not know what this meant, but they knew that the Lord lives. He then declared that he wished to preach the Lord living. But this also they refused to hear, saying that they perceived in his speech something not heavenly, because it had much regard to himself, his fame and honor, for they can tell from the very tone of one's voice whether it is from the heart, or not, and because he was such, he could not teach them. On this he was silent, for in the world he had had much pathetic power, so that he could strongly move his hearers to holiness; but this power had been acquired by art, and thus it was from himself and the world, and not from heaven.

163 They said further, that they have a perception whether the conjugial exists with those of their nation who are naked; and it was shown that they perceive this from a spiritual idea of marriage, which was communicated to me, to the effect that a similarity of interiors is formed by the conjunction of good and truth, thus of love and faith, and from that conjunction flowing down into the body conjugial love exists. For all things of the mind are presented in a certain natural appearance in the body, thus in the appearance of conjugial love, when the interiors of two mutually love each other, and from that love desire also to will and to think the one like the other, and so to be together and to be conjoined as to the interiors which are of the mind. Thus spiritual affection, which is of the minds, becomes natural affection in the body, and clothes itself with the sense of conjugial love. The spiritual affection which is of their minds is the affection of good and truth, and their conjunction; for all things of the mind, or of the thought and will, have relation to truth and good. They said also that what is given between one man and several wives is not at all conjugial, since the marriage of good and truth, which is of the minds, can be given only between two.

164 The spirit mentioned above then came to those who were naked, but with bodies inflamed, and at last to those that were black, of whom some were naked, and some clothed; but these different people dwelt in different places on the same earth, for a spirit can be led in a moment to remote parts of an earth, since he does not proceed and is not borne, as a man is, through spaces, but through changes of state (see above, n. 125, 127).[3]

165 At length I spoke with the spirits of that earth about the belief of the inhabitants of our earth concerning the resurrection, that they cannot conceive of men's coming into the other life immediately after death, and then appearing like men as to face, body, arms, feet, and all the senses, both external and internal; and still less of their being then clothed with garments and having mansions and dwellings. And the reason is that most of them there think from the sensual things which are of the body, and therefore believe in the existence of nothing which they do not see and touch. And few of them can be drawn away from external sensual things to what is interior, and so be elevated into the light of heaven in which such interior things are perceived. Hence it is, that in regard to their soul or spirit they cannot have any idea of it as a man, but as of wind, air, or breath, without form, in which there is yet something vital. This is why they do not believe they are to rise until the end of the world, which they call the Last Judgment; when they believe the body, though fallen into dust and dissipated to all the winds, will be brought back and joined to its soul and spirit. I added that they are permitted to believe this, for the reason that those who think from what is external and sensual, as has been said, can form no other idea than that one's soul or spirit can live as a man in the human form, only by regaining the body which it bore about in the world. And therefore, unless it were said that this

---

[3] Movements, progressions, and changes of place in the other life are changes of state of the interiors of the life, and still they appear to spirits and angels as real changes of place (n. 1273-1277, 1377, 3356, 5605, 10,734).

would rise again, they would reject in heart the doctrine of a resurrection and eternal life, as incomprehensible. But still that thought about the resurrection has this use in it, that they believe in a life after death, from which belief it follows that when they lie sick in bed and do not think as before from what is worldly and corporeal, thus not from things sensual, they then believe that they shall live immediately after death. They also speak then about heaven, and about the hope of living there immediately after death, laying aside their doctrine about the Last Judgment. I told these spirits further, that I sometimes wondered that when those who are in faith speak of the life after death, and of their friends who are dying or who have died, and do not at the same time think of the Last Judgment, they believe that they will live as men immediately after death. But this idea, as soon as the thought of the Last Judgment flows in, is changed into a material idea about their earthly body, that it is to be again joined to its soul. For they do not know that every man is a spirit as to his interiors, and that it is the spirit which lives in the body and in all its parts, and not the body of itself; and that it is from the spirit of every one that the body has its human form, and thus it is the spirit which is chiefly the man, and in a similar form, but invisible to the eyes of the body, yet visible to the eyes of spirits. Hence also when the sight of a man's spirit is opened, which takes place by the removal of the sight of the body, angels appear as men. Thus did the angels appear to the ancients, as related in the Word. I have also spoken sometimes with spirits whom I knew when they lived as men in the world, and have asked them whether they wished to be clothed again with their earthly body, as they had once thought. On hearing which, at the mere idea of conjunction with the body they fled away, being struck with amazement that in the world they should have thus thought from blind faith without any understanding.

166 Moreover, their dwellings on that earth were seen by me, and were long low houses, with windows on the sides according to the number of rooms or chambers into which they were divided. The roof was arched, and there was a door on each side at the end. They said that they were built of earth and roofed with sods, and the windows of threads of grass, so woven together that the light shone through. Children were also seen. And they said that their neighbors visited them, especially for the sake of their children, that they might be in company with other children, under the sight and auspices of their parents. There also appeared fields then whitening with the nearly ripened harvest. The seeds or grains of this harvest were shown, and they were like the grains of Chinese wheat. We were shown also loaves made of the grain, which were small in size and square in form. Moreover there also appeared grassy plains, with flowers therein, and trees with fruits similar to pomegranates; also shrubs, which were not vines, yet bearing berries from which wine is prepared.

167 Their sun which to us is a star, appears flaming there, and about one-fourth as large as our own sun. In their year are about two hundred days, and the days of fifteen hours length, as compared with the days on our earth. The earth itself is among the smallest in the starry heavens, being scarcely five hundred German miles[4] in circumference. This I learned from angels by comparison with such things as they saw in me, or in my memory, in relation to our earth. They formed these conclusions by angelic ideas, by which the measures of spaces and times are immediately known in their just relation to the spaces and times elsewhere. In such comparisons angelic ideas, which are spiritual, immensely exceed human idea which are natural.

---

[4] Or two thousand English geographical miles. [Translator's note]

FOURTEEN

A Fifth Earth in the Starry Heaven

168 I WAS LED AGAIN TO ANOTHER EARTH WHICH IS IN THE universe out of our solar system, and this also by changes of state, continued for nearly twelve hours. There were in company with me several spirits and angels from our earth, with whom I discoursed in the way or in that progression. I was carried at times obliquely upwards and obliquely downwards, continually towards the right, which in the other life is towards the south. In only two places I saw spirits, and in one I spoke with them. In the way or progression I was enabled to observe how immense is the Lord's heaven, which is for angels and spirits; for from the parts uninhabited I was led to conclude that it was so immense, that if there were many myriads of earths, and on each earth a multitude of men as great as in ours, there would still be a place of abode for them to eternity, and it would never be filled. This I was enabled to conclude from a comparison made with the extent of the heaven which is about our earth and designed for it, which extent was respectively so small, that it did not equal a hundred millionth part of the extent uninhabited.

169 When the angelic spirits who were from that earth came into view, they accosted us, asking who we were, and what we wanted. We said that we came for the sake of journeying, that we were directed thither, and that they had nothing to fear from us; for they were afraid we were of those who disturb them in regard to God, to faith, and things of a like nature, on account of whom they had betaken themselves to that quarter of their earth, shunning them as much as possible. We asked them by what they were disturbed. They replied, by an idea of three, and by an idea of the Divine without the Human, in God, when yet they know and perceive that God is one, and that He is Man. It was then perceived that they who disturbed them, and whom they shunned, were from our earth. This was manifest also from this, that there are from our earth those who thus wander about in the other life in consequence of their fondness for and delight in travelling, which they have contracted in the world; for on other earths there is no such custom of travelling as on ours. It was then discovered that they were monks, who had traveled on our globe from the zeal of converting the Gentiles; wherefore we told them they did well to shun them, because their intention was not to teach, but to secure gain and dominion; and that they study by various arts first to captivate men's minds, but afterwards to subject them to themselves as slaves. Moreover, that they did well in not suffering their ideas concerning God to be disturbed by such. They said further, that the above spirits confuse them by asserting that they ought to have faith and to believe the things they say; but they replied to them, that they know not what faith is nor what is meant by believing, since they perceive in themselves whether a thing be true or not. They were of the Lord's celestial kingdom, where all know from an interior perception the truths which with us are called the truths of faith, for they are in enlightenment from the Lord; but it is otherwise with those who are in the spiritual kingdom. That the angelic spirits of that earth were of the Lord's celestial kingdom, it was granted me to see from the flaming light whence their ideas flowed; for the light in the celestial kingdom is flaming, and in the spiritual kingdom it is white. They who are of the celestial kingdom, when the discourse is about truths, say no more than yea, yea, or nay, nay, and never reason about truths whether they be so or not so. These are they of whom the Lord speaks:

> Let your discourse be yea, yea, and nay, nay, for whatsoever is more than this is from evil.

Hence it was that those spirits said that they did not know what is meant by having faith or believing. They consider this, like a person's saying to his companion who sees houses or trees with his own eyes, that he ought to have faith or to believe that they are houses and trees, when he sees clearly that they are so. Such are they who are of the Lord's celestial kingdom, and such were these angelic spirits.[1] We told them that there are few on our earth who have interior perception, because in their youth they learn truths and do not do them. For man has two faculties, which are called the understanding and the will; they who admit truths no further than into the memory, and thence in some small degree into the understanding, and not into the life, that is, into the will, these, inasmuch as they are not capable of any enlightenment or interior sight from the Lord, say that those truths are to be believed, or that they are objects of faith, and also reason concerning them whether they be truths or not; yea, they are not willing that they should be perceived by any interior sight, or by any enlightenment in the understanding. They say this, because truths with them are without light from heaven, and to those who see without light from heaven, falsities may appear like truths, and truths like falsities; hence so great blindness has seized many there, that although they do not do truths or live according to them, still they say that they can be saved by faith alone, as if it were the knowledge of the things of faith which constitutes man, and not the life according to that knowledge. We afterwards discoursed with them concerning the Lord, concerning love to Him, concerning love toward the neighbor, and concerning regeneration; saying that to love the Lord is to love the commandments which are from Him, which

---

[1] Heaven is distinguished into two kingdoms, one of which is called the celestial kingdom, the other the spiritual kingdom (n. 3887, 4138). The angels in the celestial kingdom know innumerable things and are immensely more wise than the angels in the spiritual kingdom (n. 2718). The celestial angels do not think and speak from faith, like the spiritual angels, but from an internal perception that a thing is so (n. 202, 597, 607, 784, 1121, 1387, 1398, 1442, 1919, 7680, 7877, 8780). The celestial angels say only concerning the truths of faith, yea, yea, or nay, nay, but the spiritual angels reason whether it be so or not so (n. 202, 337, 2715, 3246, 4448, 9196)

is to live according to them from love.[2] That love toward the neighbor is to will good and thence do good to a fellow-citizen, to one's country, to the church, and to the Lord's kingdom, not for the sake of self, to be seen, or to merit, but from the affection of good.[3] Concerning regeneration, we observed that they who are regenerated by the Lord, and commit truths immediately to life, come into an interior perception concerning them; but that they who receive truths first in the memory, and afterwards will them and do them, are they who are in faith; for they act from faith, which is then called conscience. They said that they perceived these things to be so, and thus perceived also what faith is. I discoursed with them by spiritual ideas, whereby such things may be exhibited and comprehended in light.

170 The spirits with whom I now discoursed were from the northern part of their earth. I was afterwards led to others who were on the western part. These also, wishing to discover who and what I was, immediately said that there was nothing in me but evil, thinking thus to deter me from approaching nearer. It was perceived that this was their manner of accosting all who came to them; but it was granted me to reply that I well knew it to be so, and that with them also there was nothing but evil, by reason that every one is born in evil, and therefore whatever comes from man, spirit, and angel, as from what is his own, or his proprium, is nothing but evil, inasmuch as all good with every one is from the Lord. Hence they perceived that I was in the truth, and I was admitted to speak with them. They then showed me their idea concerning evil with man, and concerning good from the Lord, how they are separated from each other. They placed one near the other, almost contiguous, but still distinct, yet as it were bound together in a manner inexpressible, so that the good led the evil, and restrained it, insomuch that it was not allowed it to act at pleasure; and thus the good bent the evil in whatever direction desired, without the evil knowing it. In this manner they exhibited the dominion of good over evil, and at the same time a state

---

[2] To love the Lord is to live according to His commandments (n. 10,143, 10,153, 10,310, 10,578, 10,648).

[3] To love the neighbor is to do what is good, just, and right, in every work and in every function, from the affection of what is good, just, and right (n. 8120-8122, 10,310, 10,336). A life of love towards the neighbor is a life according to the Lord's commandments (n. 3249

of freedom. They then asked how the Lord appeared with the angels from our earth. I said that He appears in the sun as Man, encompassed therein with solar fire, whence the angels in the heavens have all light; and that the heat which proceeds thence is the Divine good, and that the light which proceeds thence is the Divine truth, each from the Divine love, which is the fire appearing around the Lord in that sun. That sun, however, appears only to the angels in heaven, and not to the spirits who are beneath, since they are more removed from the reception of the good of love and of the truth of faith, than the angels who are in the heavens (see above, n. 40). It was granted them thus to inquire concerning the Lord, and concerning His appearance before the angels from our earth, because it then pleased the Lord to present Himself before them, and to reduce into order the things which had been disturbed by the evil spirits of whom they complained. This also was the reason why I was led thither, that I might see these things.

171 There was then seen a dark cloud toward the east, descending from on high, which in descending gradually appeared bright and in the human form; and this form at length appeared in a flaming radiance, around which were little stars of the same color. In this manner the Lord presented Himself before the spirits with whom I was speaking. To this Presence were then gathered together from every side all the spirits who were there; and when they came, the good were separated from the evil, the good to the right and the evil to the left, and this at once, as of their own accord. And those on the right were arranged according to the quality of their good, and those on the left according to the quality of their evil. The good were then left to form a heavenly society among themselves; but the evil were cast into the hells. I saw afterward that this flaming radiance descended quite deep into the lower parts of the earth there; and then it appeared, now flamy verging to brightness, now bright verging to obscurity, and now in obscurity. And I was told by angels that the appearance is according to the reception of truth from good, and of falsity from evil, with those who inhabit the lower parts of that earth; and that the flamy radiance itself did not at all undergo such variations. They said also that the lower parts of that earth were inhabited as well by the good as by the evil; but well separated, in order that the evil might be ruled through the good by the Lord. They added that the good were by turns taken up thence into heaven by the Lord, and others succeed in their place, and so on continually. In that descent the good were in like manner separated from the evil, and all things were reduced into order. For the evil, by various arts and crafty devices, had introduced themselves into the dwellings of the good there, and infested them; and this was the cause of that visitation. That cloud, which in descending gradually appeared bright and in the human form, and then as a flamy radiance, was an angelic society, in the midst of which was the Lord. From this it was given to know what is meant by the Lord's words in the Evangelists, where He speaks of the Last Judgment:

> That He will come with the angel in the clouds of heaven
> with glory and power.

172 Afterward some monkish spirits were seen, namely, those who had been travelling monks or missionaries in the world, and who have been spoken of above; and a crowd of spirits was also seen, who were from that earth, most of them evil, whom they had drawn over and seduced to their side. These were seen at the eastern quarter of that earth, from which they drove away the good, who betook themselves to the northern side of that earth, and have been spoken of above. That crowd, together with their seducers was collected into one body, to the number of some thousands, and was separated when the evil were cast into the hells. I was granted to speak with one spirit who was a monk, and to ask what he did there. He replied that he taught them concerning the Lord. I asked, what besides. He said, concerning heaven and hell. I asked, what further. He said, concerning a belief in all that he should say. I asked, what further. He said, concerning the power of remitting sins, and of opening and shutting heaven. He was then examined as to what he knew concerning the Lord, concerning the truths of faith, concerning the remission of sins, concerning man's salvation, and concerning heaven and hell; and it was discovered that he knew scarcely anything, and that he was in obscurity and falsity concerning all and each of them, and that he was possessed solely by the lust of gain and dominion which he had contracted in the world and brought with him thence. Wherefore he was told that, because he had traveled so far led by that lust, and was such as to doctrine, he must needs deprive the spirits of that earth of celestial light, and bring in the darkness of hell, and thus bring them under the dominion of hell, and not of the Lord. Moreover he was cunning in seducing, but stupid as to those things which are of heaven. Because he was such he was then cast thence into hell. Thus the spirits of that earth were liberated from them.

173 The spirits of that earth mentioned also, among other things, that those strangers, who, as has been said, were monkish spirits, used all their endeavors to persuade them to live together in society, and not separate and solitary; for spirits and angels dwell and associate in like manner as in the world; they who have dwelt in communities in the world, dwell also in a similar state in the other life; and they who have dwelt in a separate state, divided into houses and families, dwell also in a separate state in another life. These spirits on their earth, while they lived there as men, had dwelt in a separate state, house and house, families and families, and thus nation and nation apart, and hence they knew not what it was to dwell together in society. Wherefore when it was told them that those strangers wished to persuade them to dwell in society, to the intent that they might rule and have dominion over them, and that they could not otherwise subject them to themselves and make them slaves, they replied that they were totally ignorant what was meant by ruling and domineering. That they flee away at the very idea of rule and dominion, was made manifest to me from this, that one of them, who accompanied us back again, when I showed him the city in which I dwelt, at the first sight of it fled away, and was no more seen.

174 I then spoke with the angels who were with me concerning dominion, saying that there are two kinds of dominion, one of love towards the neighbor, and the other of self-love; and that the dominion of love towards the neighbor is among those who dwell separated into houses, families, and nations; whereas the dominion of self-love is among those who dwell together in society. Among those who live separated into houses, families, and nations, he has dominion who is the father of the nation, and under him the father of families, and under these the father of each house. He is called the father of the nation from whom the families originate, from which families the houses are derived; but all these exercise dominion from love, like that of a father towards his children, who teaches them how they ought to live, does good to them, and as far as he can, gives them of his own. It never enters into his mind to subject them to himself, as subjects or as servants, but he loves that they should obey him as sons obey their father. And because this love increases in descending, as is known, therefore the father of the nation acts from a more interior love than the father himself from whom the sons are next descended. Such also is the dominion in the heavens, inasmuch as such is the Lord's dominion; for His dominion is from the Divine love towards the whole human race. But the dominion of self-love, which is opposite to the dominion of love towards the neighbor, began when man alienated himself from the Lord; for in proportion as man does not love and worship the Lord, in the same proportion he loves and worships himself, and so far also he loves the world. Then from necessity that they might be safe, the nations with their families and houses, formed themselves into one body, and established governments under various forms. For in proportion as self-love increased, in the same proportion all kinds of evil, as enmity, envy, hatred, revenge, cruelty and deceit, increased with it, being exercised against all who opposed them. For from the proprium in which they are who are in self-love, nothing but evil springs, inasmuch its man's proprium is nothing but evil, and because the proprium is evil, it does not receive good from heaven. Hence self-love, while it has dominion, is the father of all such evils.[4] And that love is also of such a nature that as far as the reins are relaxed it rushes on, until at length every one possessed by it wishes to domineer over all others in the whole world, and to possess all the goods of others. Yea, even this is

---

[4] Man's proprium, which he derives from his parents, is nothing but dense evil (n. 210, 215, 731, 874, 876, 987, 1047, 2307, 2318, 3518, 3701, 3812, 8480, 8550, 10,283, 10,284, 10,286, 10,731). Man's proprium consists in loving himself more than God, and the world more than heaven, and in making light of his neighbor in respect to himself, except it be for the sake of himself, and thus from motives of self-love and the love of the world (n. 694, 731, 4317, 5660). All evils flow from self-love and the love of the world, when they have dominion (n. 1307, 1308, 1321, 1594, 1691, 3413, 7255, 7376, 7480, 7488, 8318, 9335, 9348, 10,038, 10,742). These evils are contempt of others, enmity, hatred, revenge, cruelty, and deceit (n. 6667, 7372-7374, 9348, 10,038, 10,742). And that from these evils every falsity flows (n. 1047, 10,283, 10,284, 10,286).

not enough, but he wishes to have dominion over the whole heaven, as may be evident from the Babylon of this day. This then is the rule of self-love, from which the rule of the love of the neighbor differs as much as heaven does from hell. But however great such dominion of self-love is in societies or in kingdoms and empires, still even in these is found also the dominion of love towards the neighbor among those who are wise from faith in and love to God; for these love the neighbor. That these also dwell in the heavens distinguished into nations, families, and houses, although in societies together, but according to spiritual affinities, which are those of the good of love and the truth of faith, will by the Divine mercy of the Lord be told elsewhere.

175 I afterward questioned those spirits about various things on the earth from which they were, and first about their Divine worship and revelation. In regard to worship they said that the nations with their families assemble at one place every thirtieth day, and hear preaching; and that the preacher then, from a pulpit raised a little above the earth, teaches them Divine truths, which lead to the good of life. Concerning revelation they said that it came in the early morning, in a state midway between sleep and wakefulness, when they are in interior light not yet interrupted by the bodily senses and by worldly things. And that they then hear angels of heaven speaking of Divine truths, and of a life according to them; that when they awaken, an angel in a white garment appears to them by the bed, who then suddenly disappears from their sight; and that from this they know that what they have heard is from heaven. In this way Divine vision is distinguished from vision not Divine; for in vision not Divine no angel appears. They added that revelations are made in this manner to their preachers, also sometimes to others.

176 To an inquiry concerning their houses, they said that they are low, of wood, with a flat roof, around which project caves sloping downward; and that in the front part dwell the husband and wife, in the next adjoining part the children, and after them the maidservants and men-servants. Of their food they said that they drink milk with water, and that they have the milk from cows, which are woolly like sheep. Of their life they said that they walk naked, and that to them nakedness is not a cause of shame; also that their social intercourse is with those who are within their families.

177 In regard to the sun of that earth they related that to the inhabitants it has a flamy appearance; that the length of their years is two hundred days, and that a day equals nine hours of our time, which they could conclude from the length of the days of our earth perceived in me. And further, that they have perpetual spring and summer, and consequently that the fields are ever green, and the trees ever bearing fruit. The reason of this is, because their year is so short, being equal only to seventy-five days of our year; and when the years are so short, the cold does not continue long in winter nor the heat in summer, whence the ground is continually verdant.

178 Concerning betrothals and marriages in that earth, they related that a daughter, when she arrives at a marriageable age, is kept at home, nor is she allowed to leave the house till the day she is to be married; that then she is conducted to a certain connubial house, where there are also many other young women of marriageable age brought together, and there they are placed behind a screen, which reaches to the middle of the body, so that they appear naked as to the breast and face: and that then the young men come thither to choose for themselves a wife. And when a young man sees one that seems suited to him, and to whom his mind draws him, he takes her by the hand; and if she then follows him, he leads her to a house prepared, and she becomes his wife. For they see from the face whether they agree in mind, inasmuch as there every one's face is an index of the mind, and in nothing does it dissemble and deceive. That all things may be done decently and without lasciviousness, an old man is seated behind the virgins, and an old woman at the side of them, to make their observations. There are many such places to which the young women are conducted: and also stated times for the young men to make their choice. For if they do not find a maid to suit them in one place, they go to another; and if not at one time, they return again at a future time. They said further, that a husband has only one wife, and never more than one, because this is contrary to Divine order.